This Coloring Book Belongs To

_____

_____

_____

_____

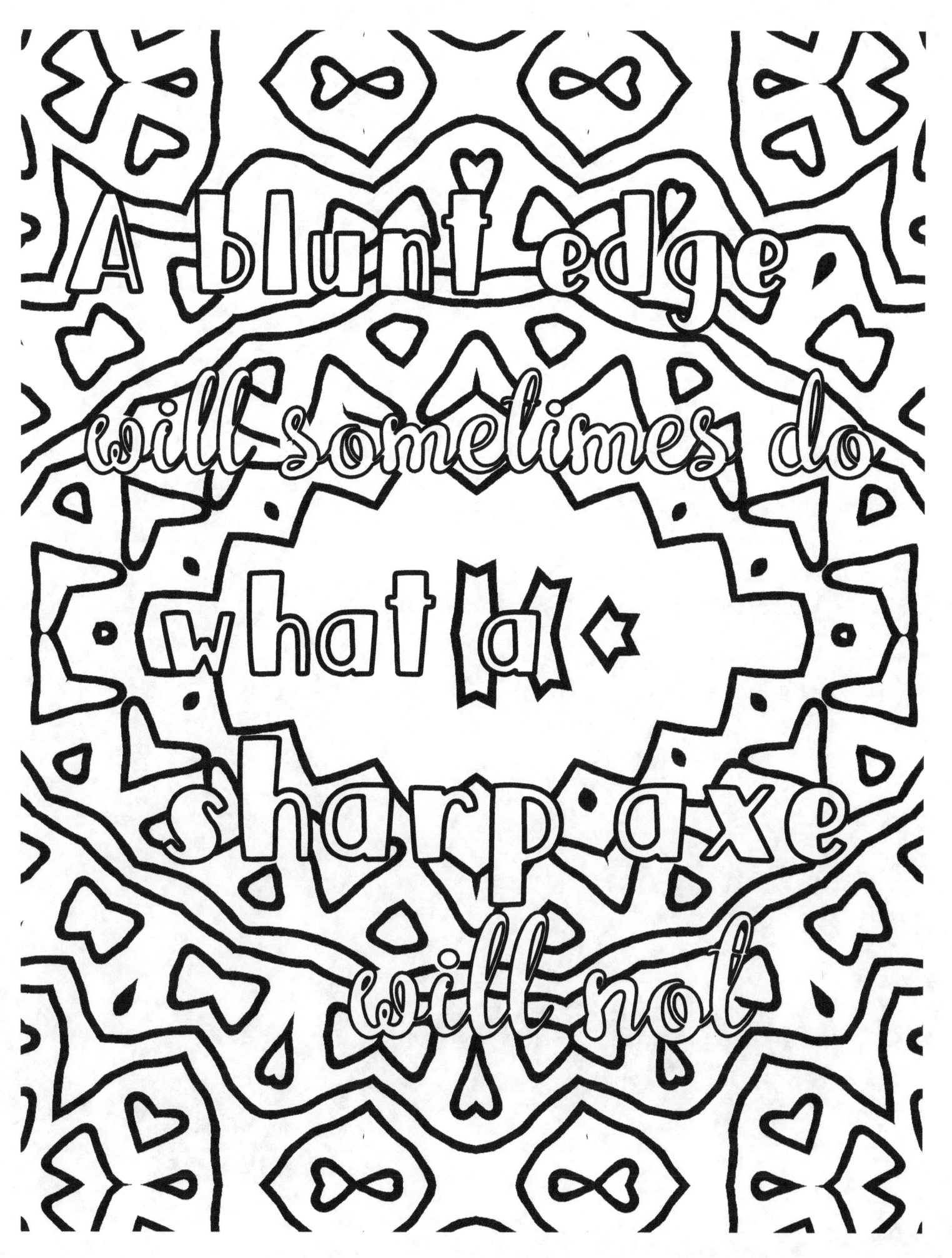

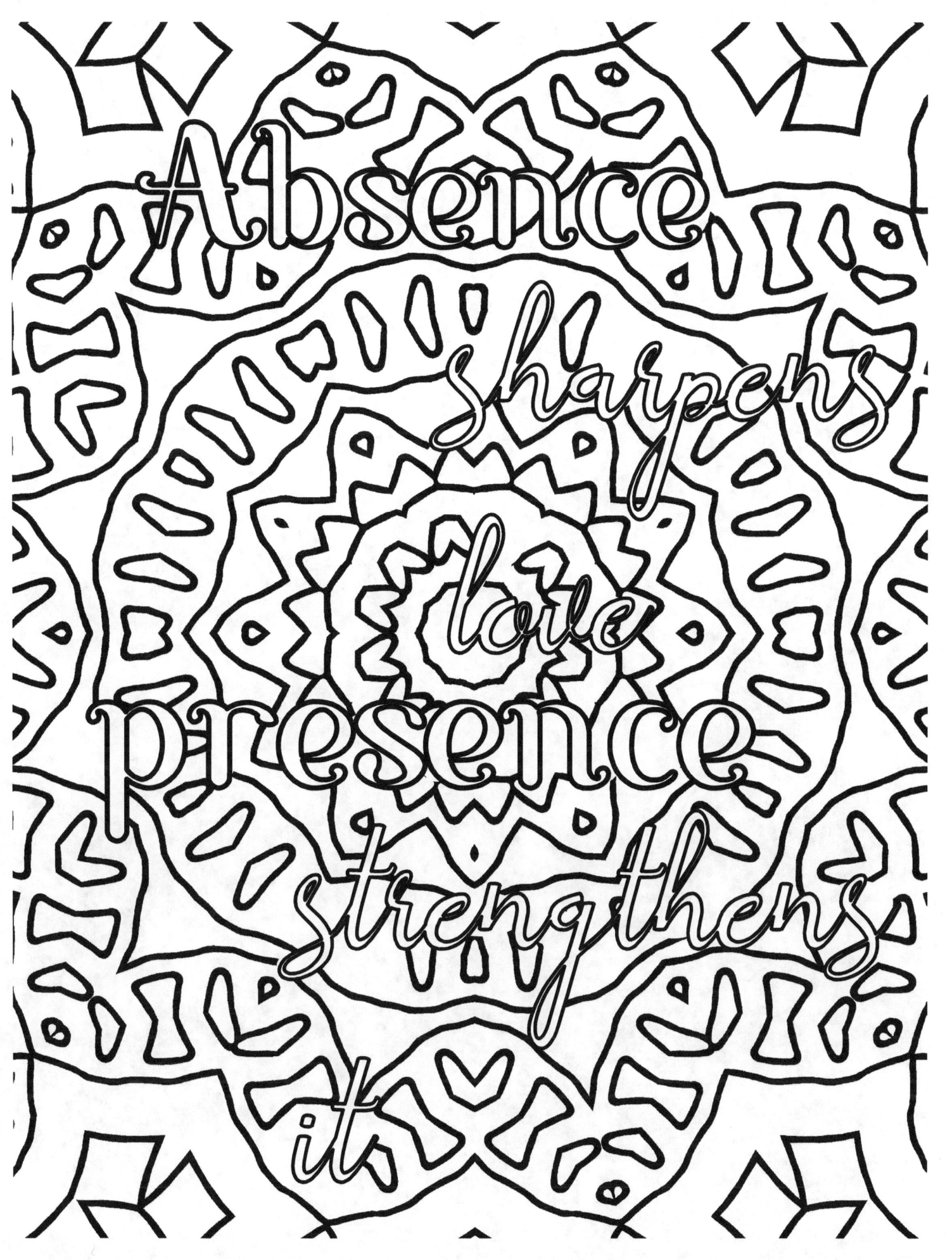

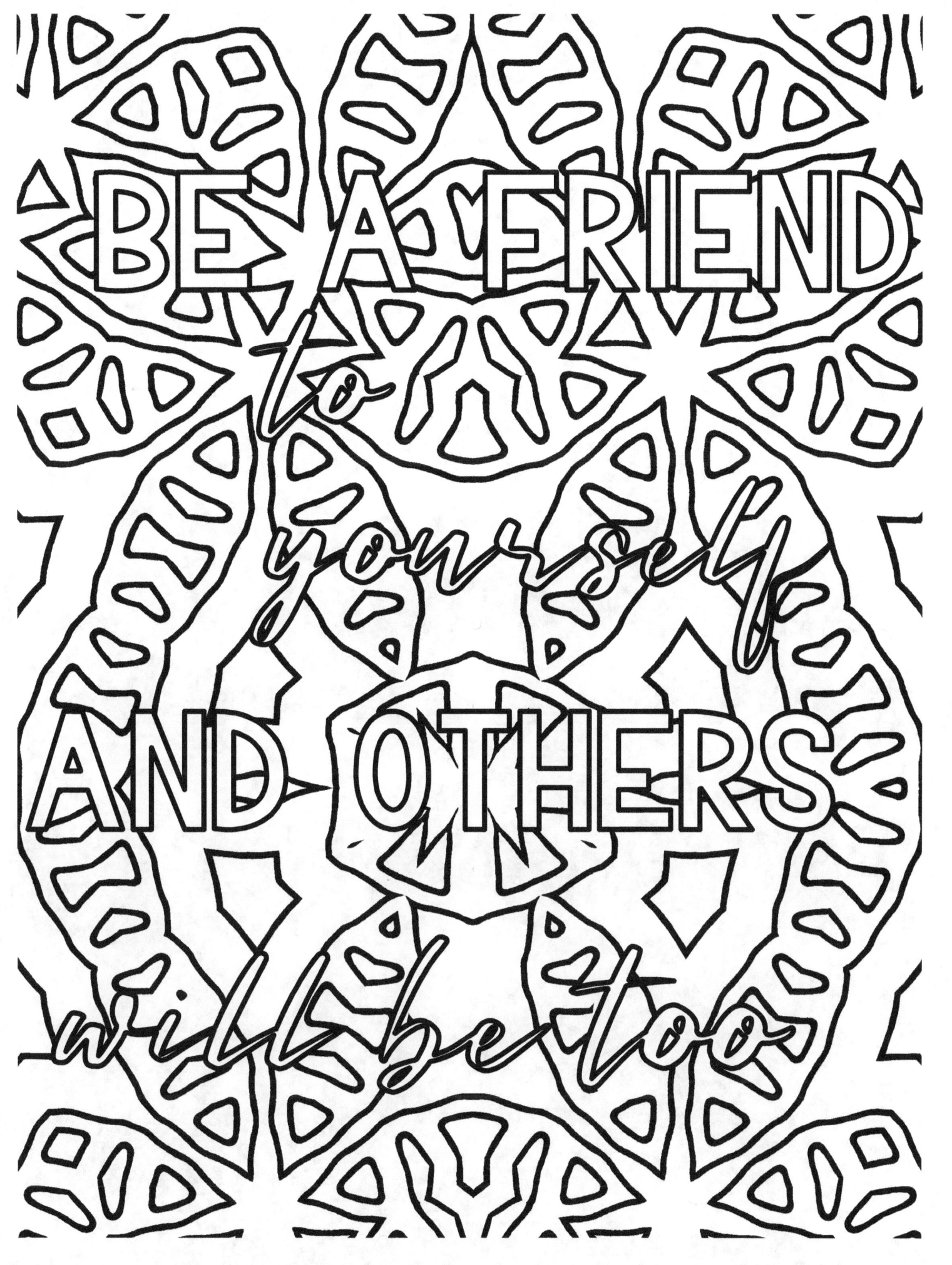

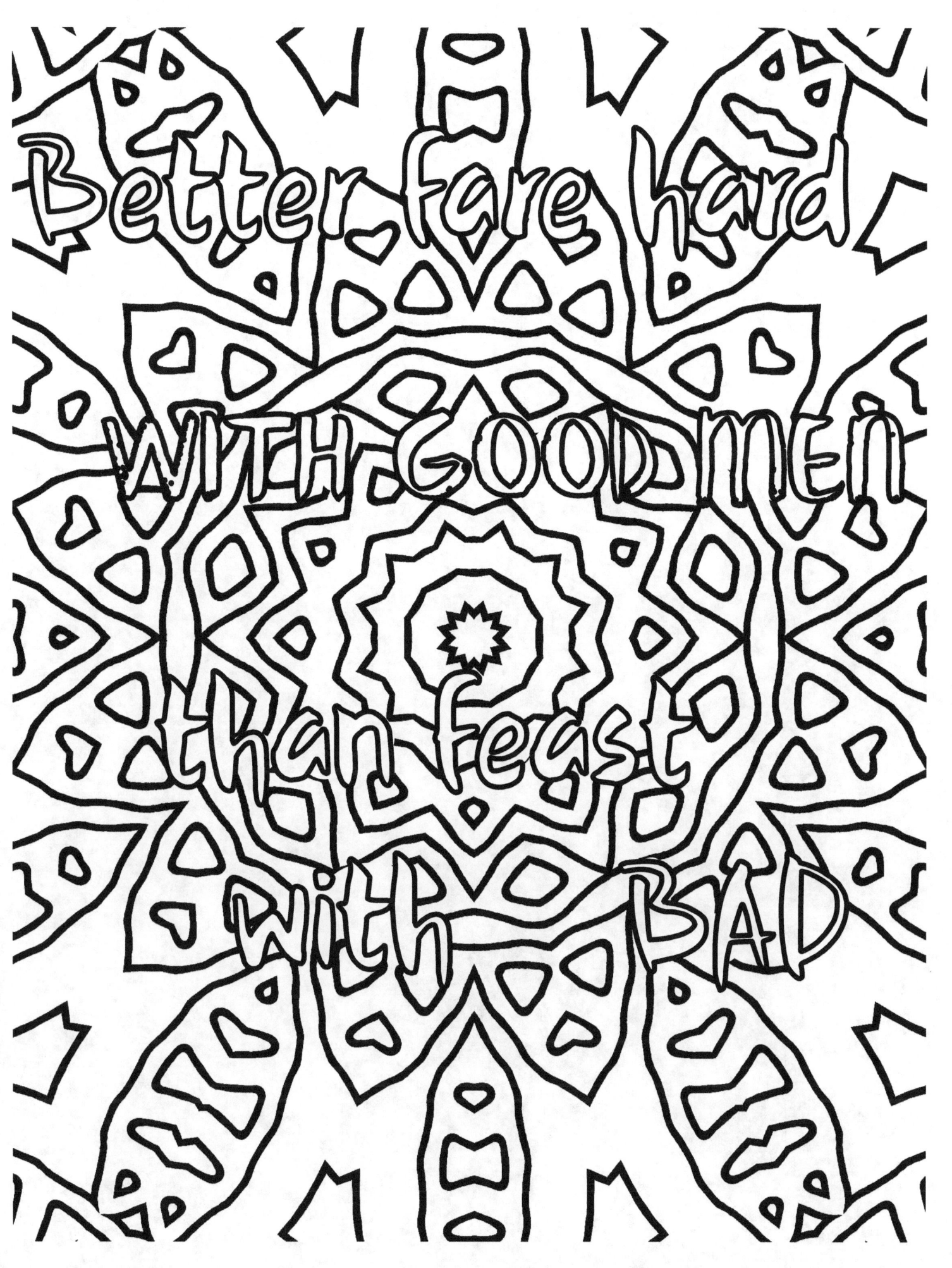

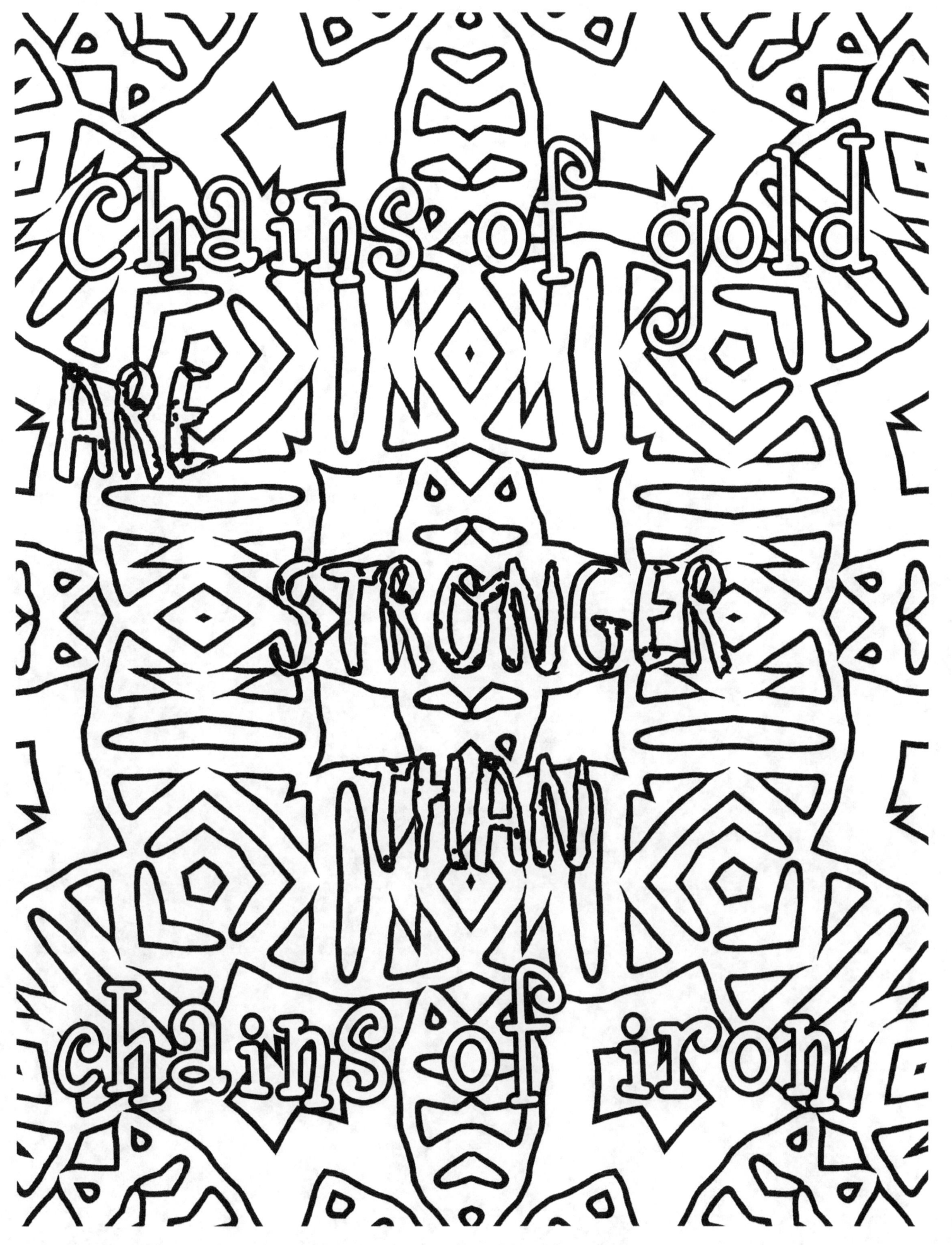

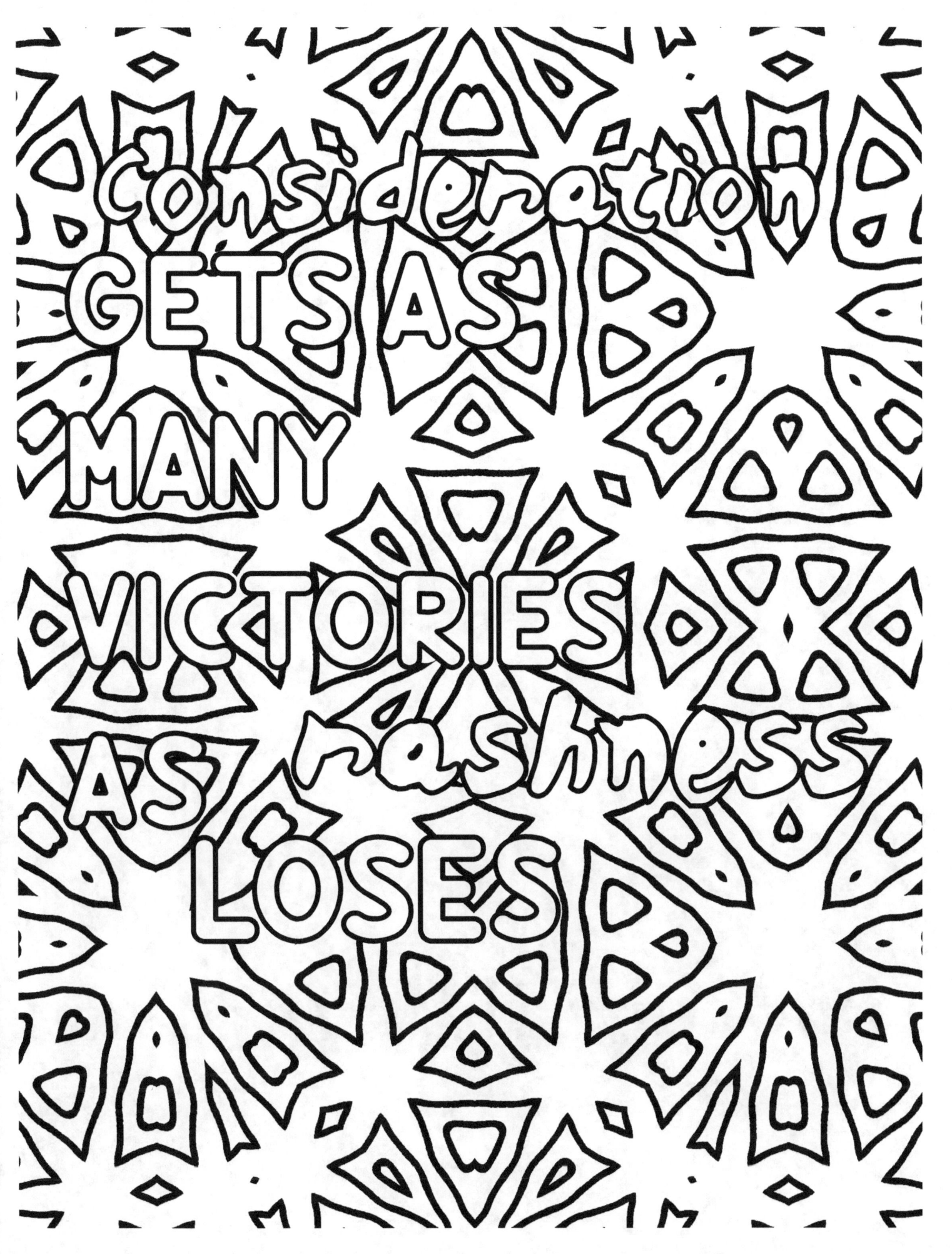

Consideration GETS AS MANY VICTORIES AS rashness LOSES

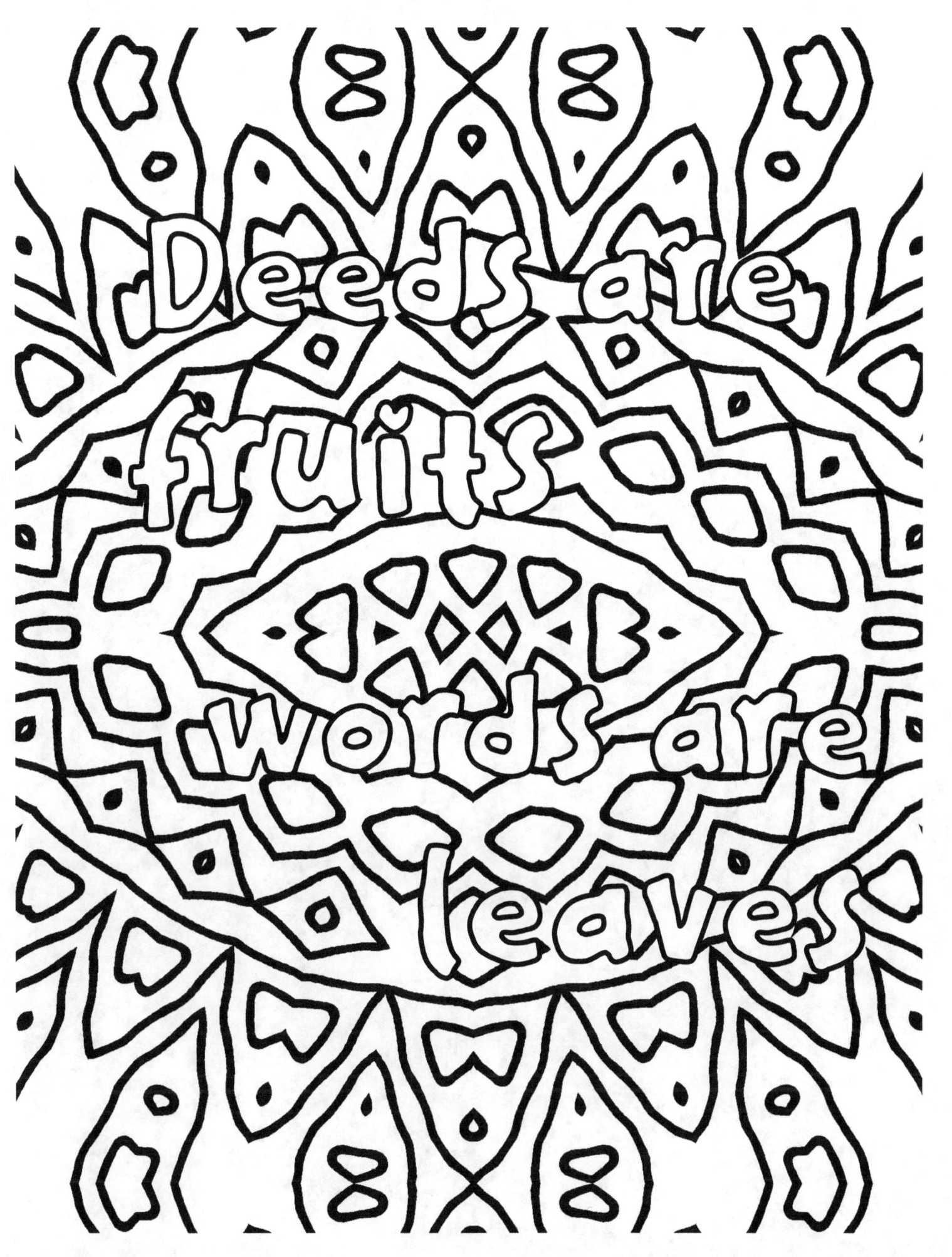

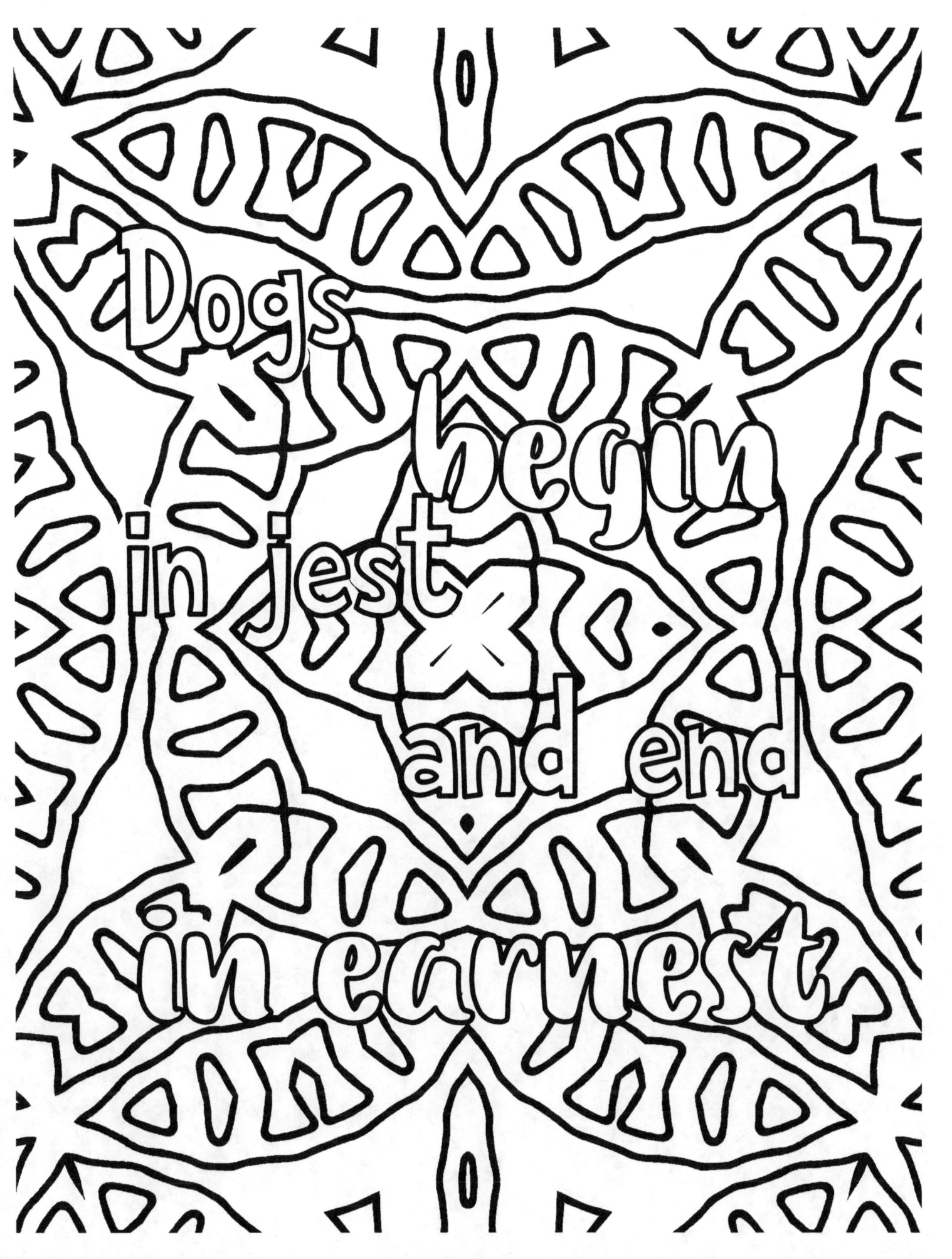

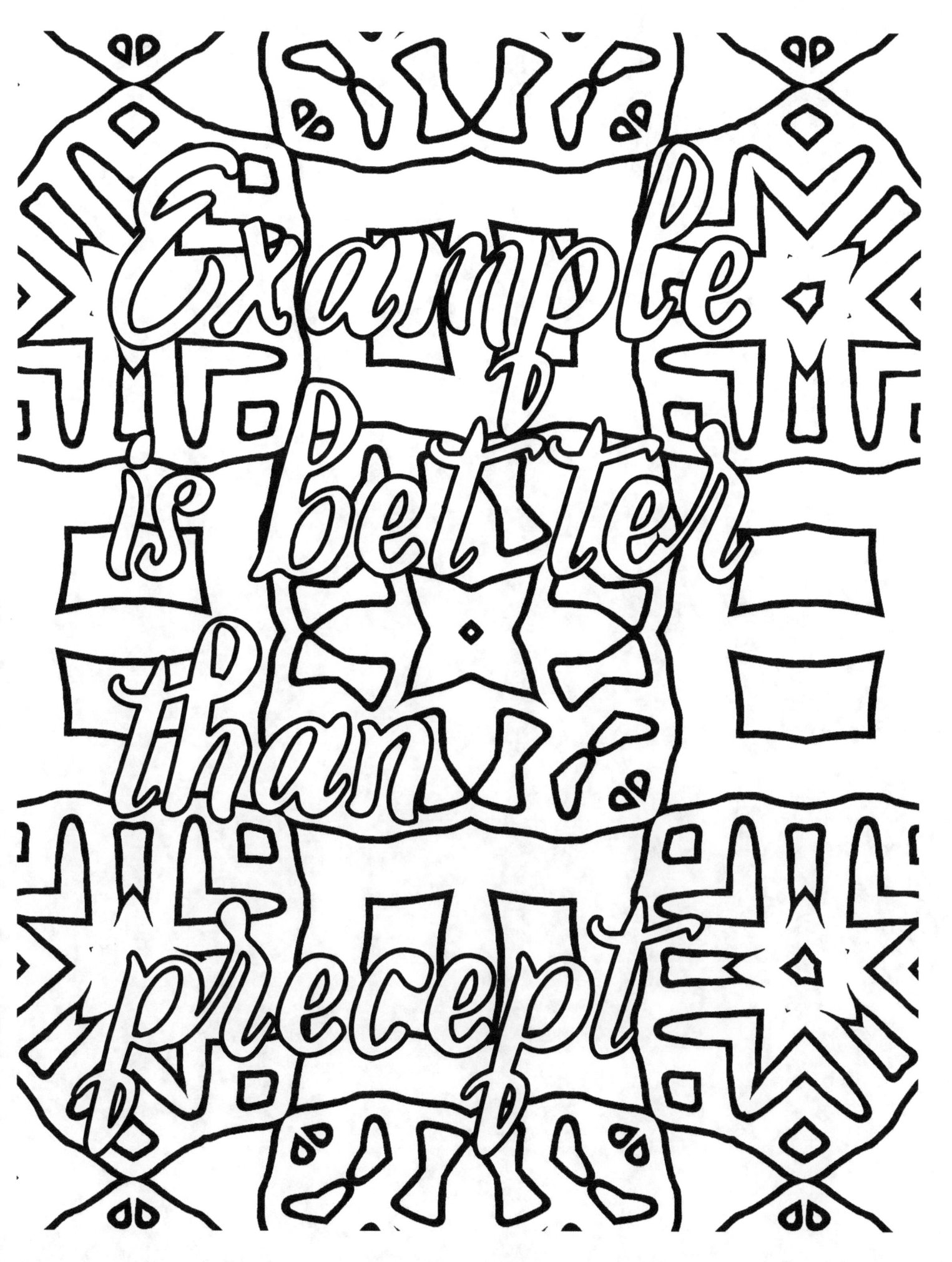

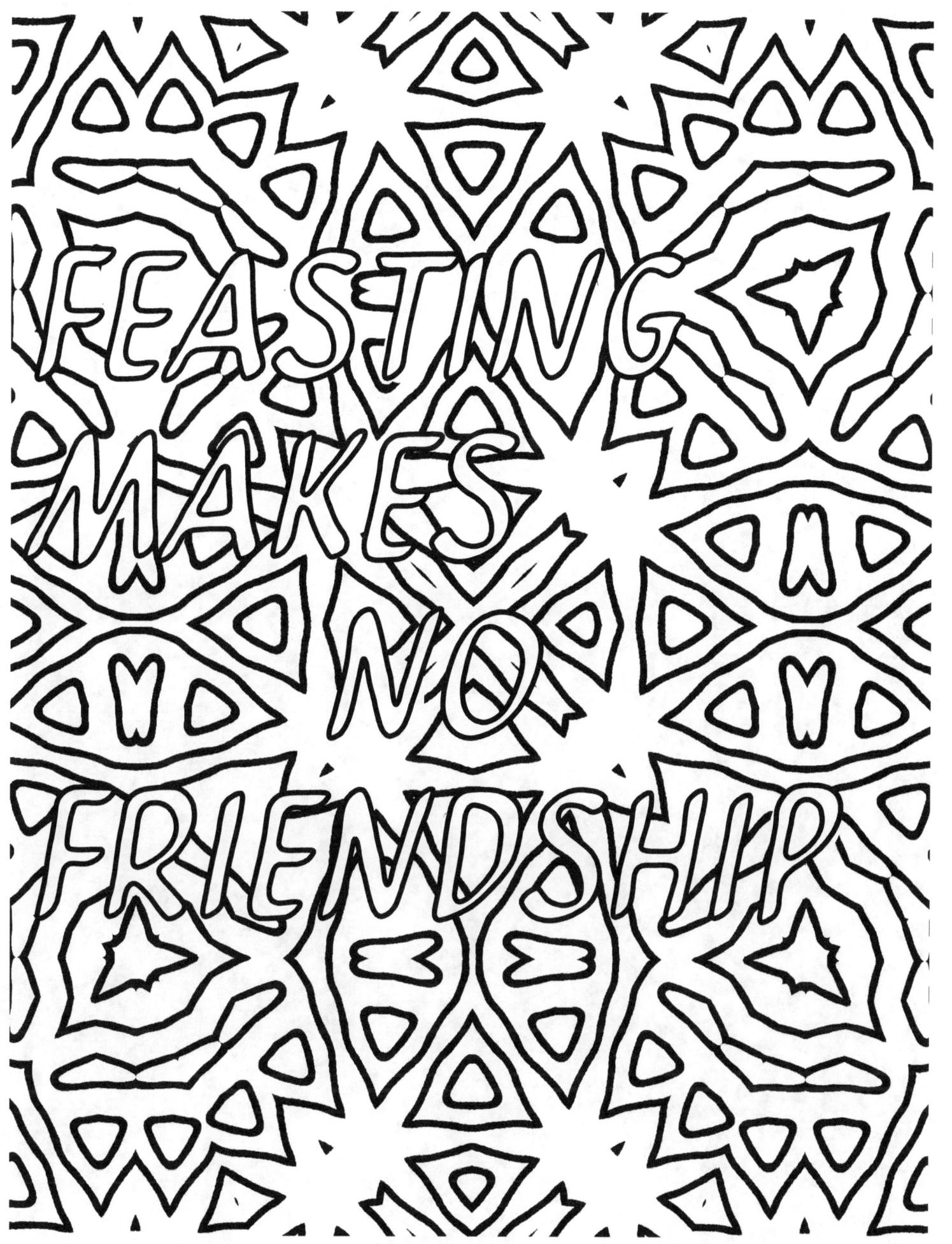

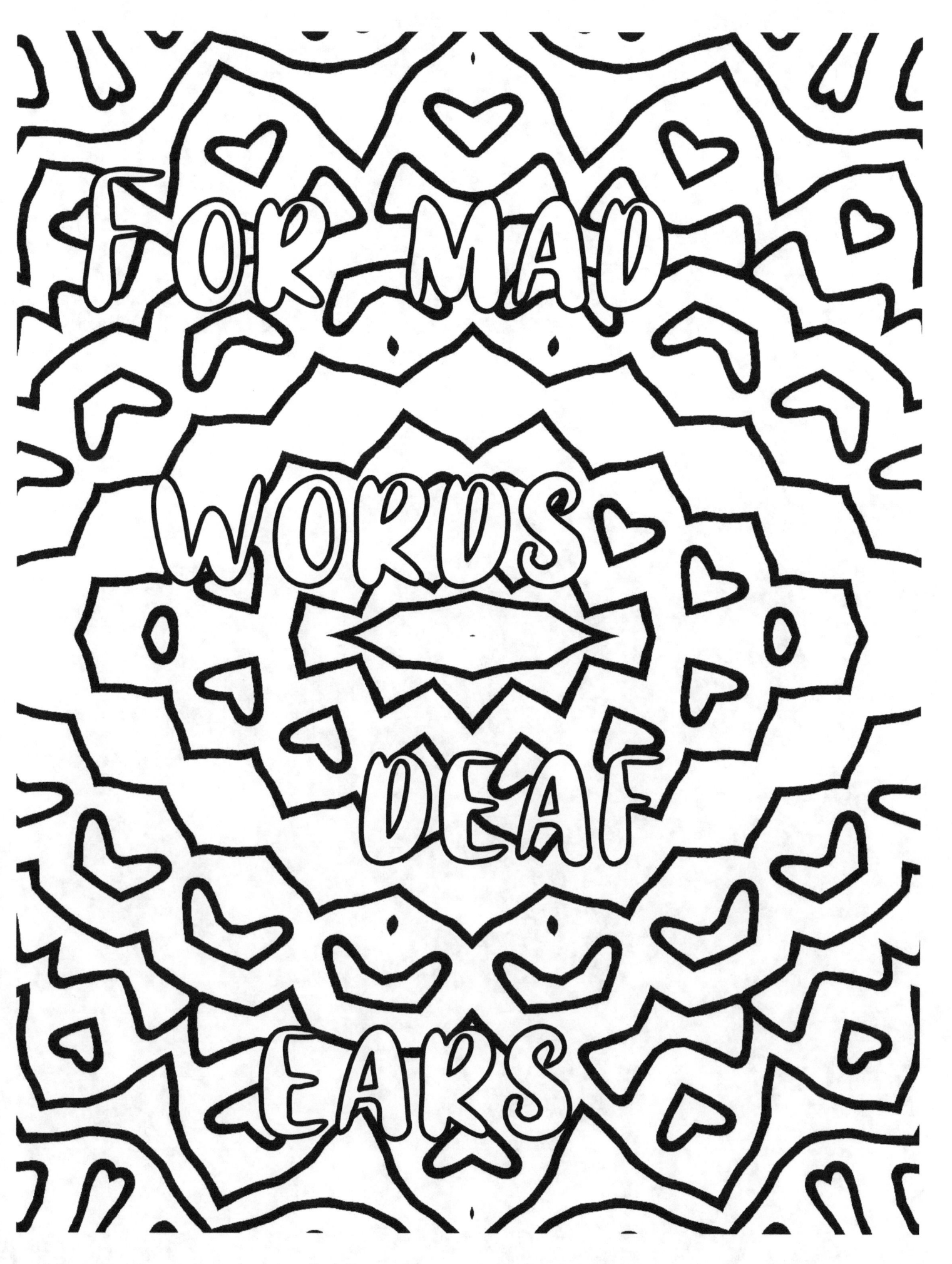

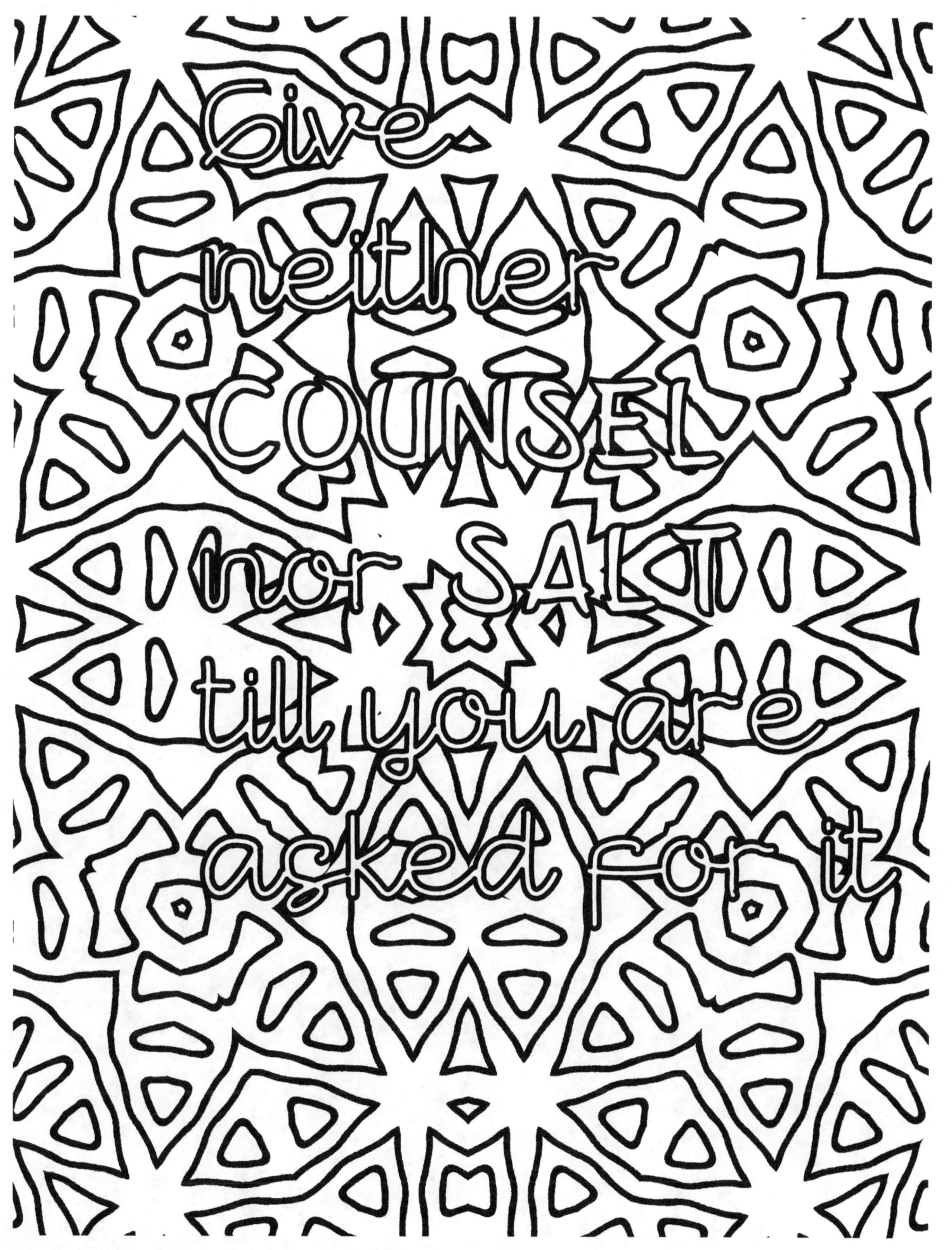

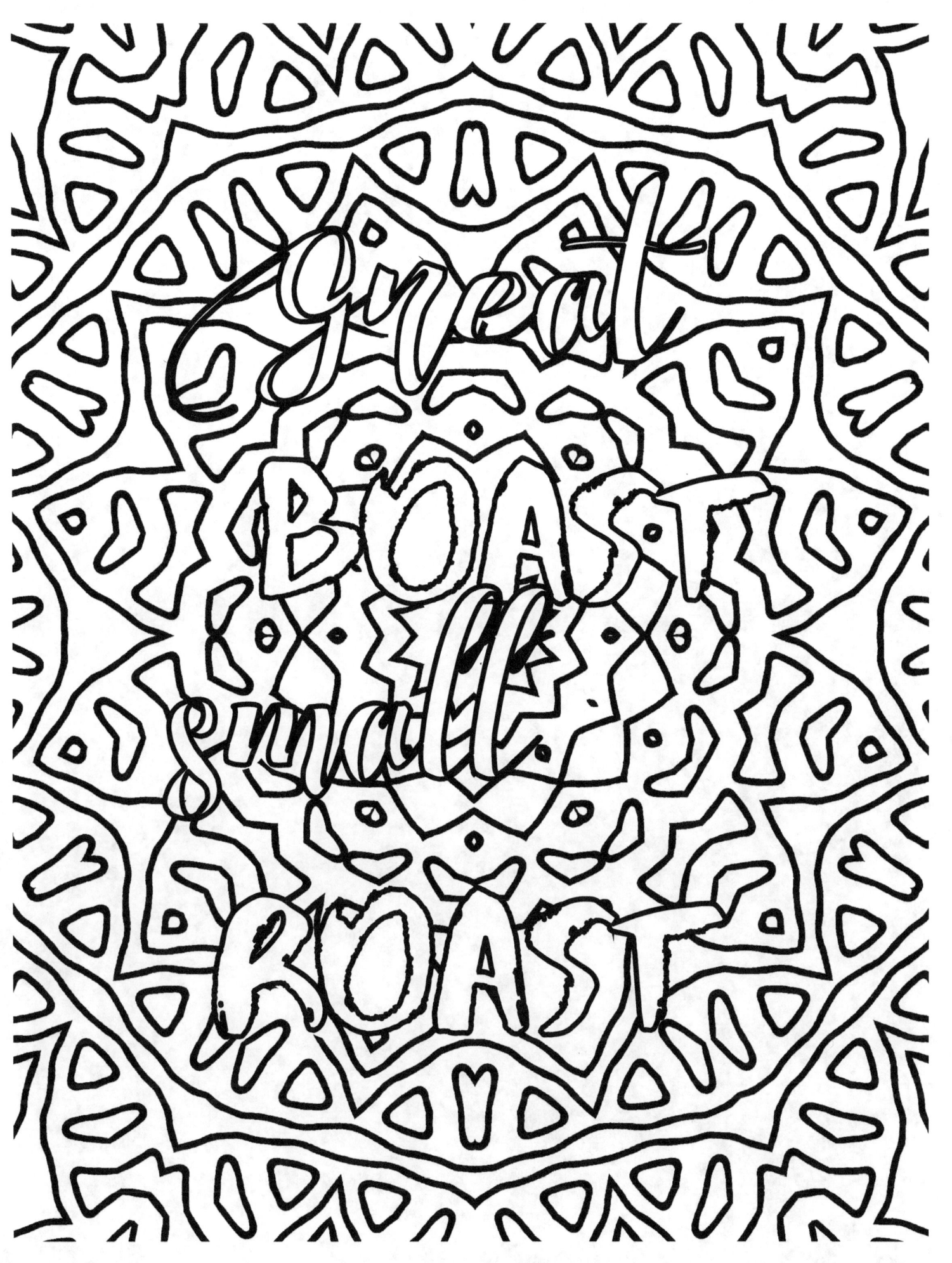

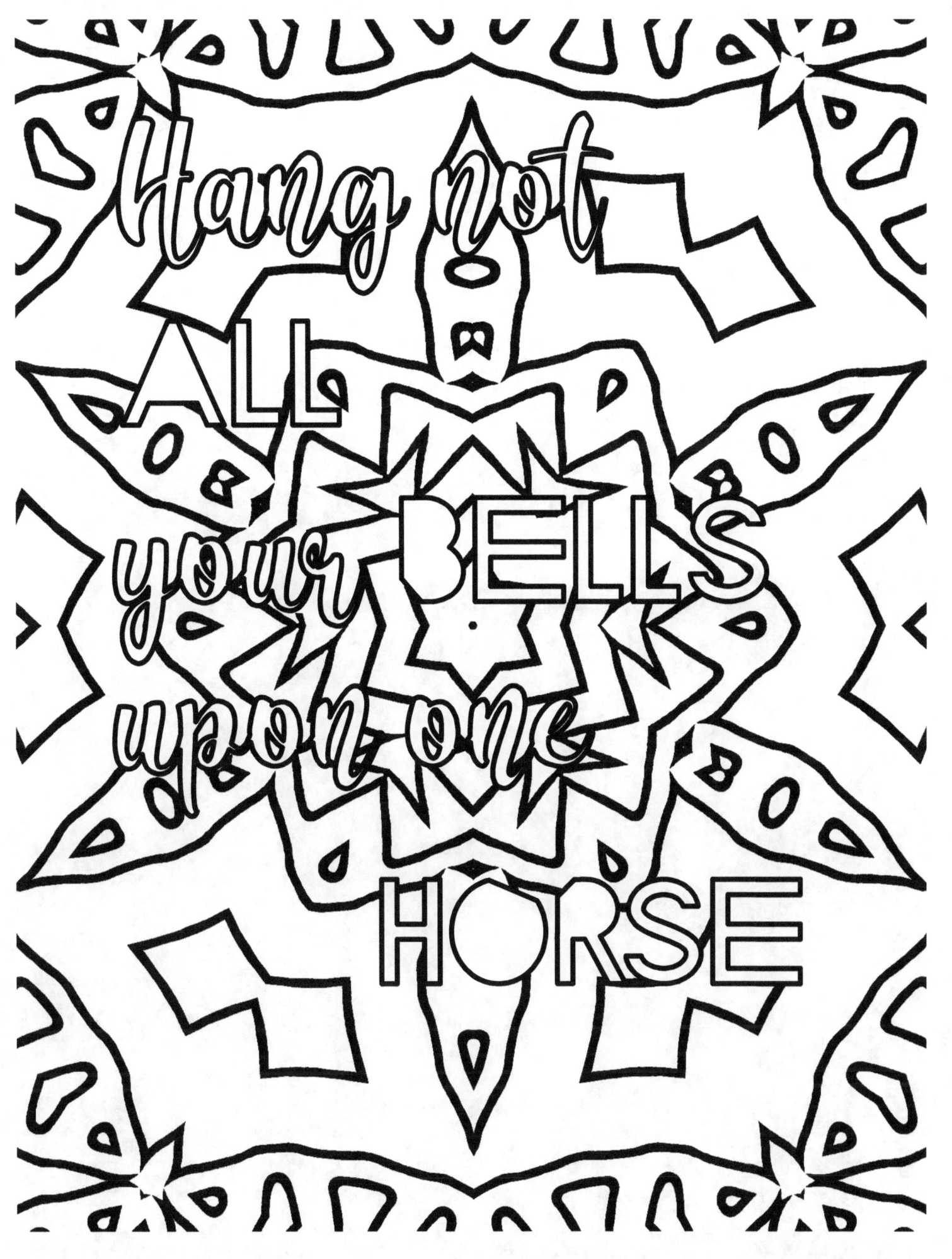

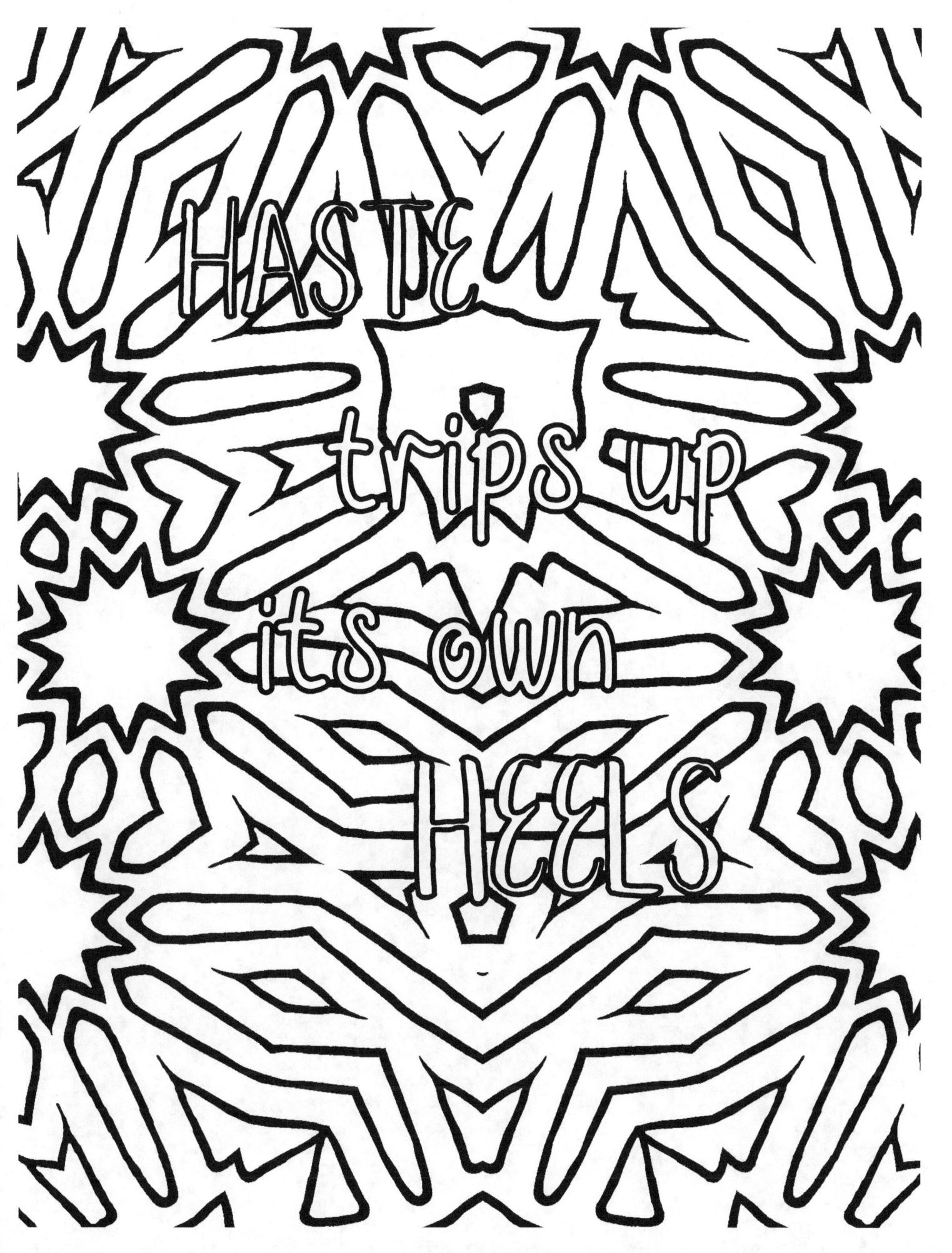

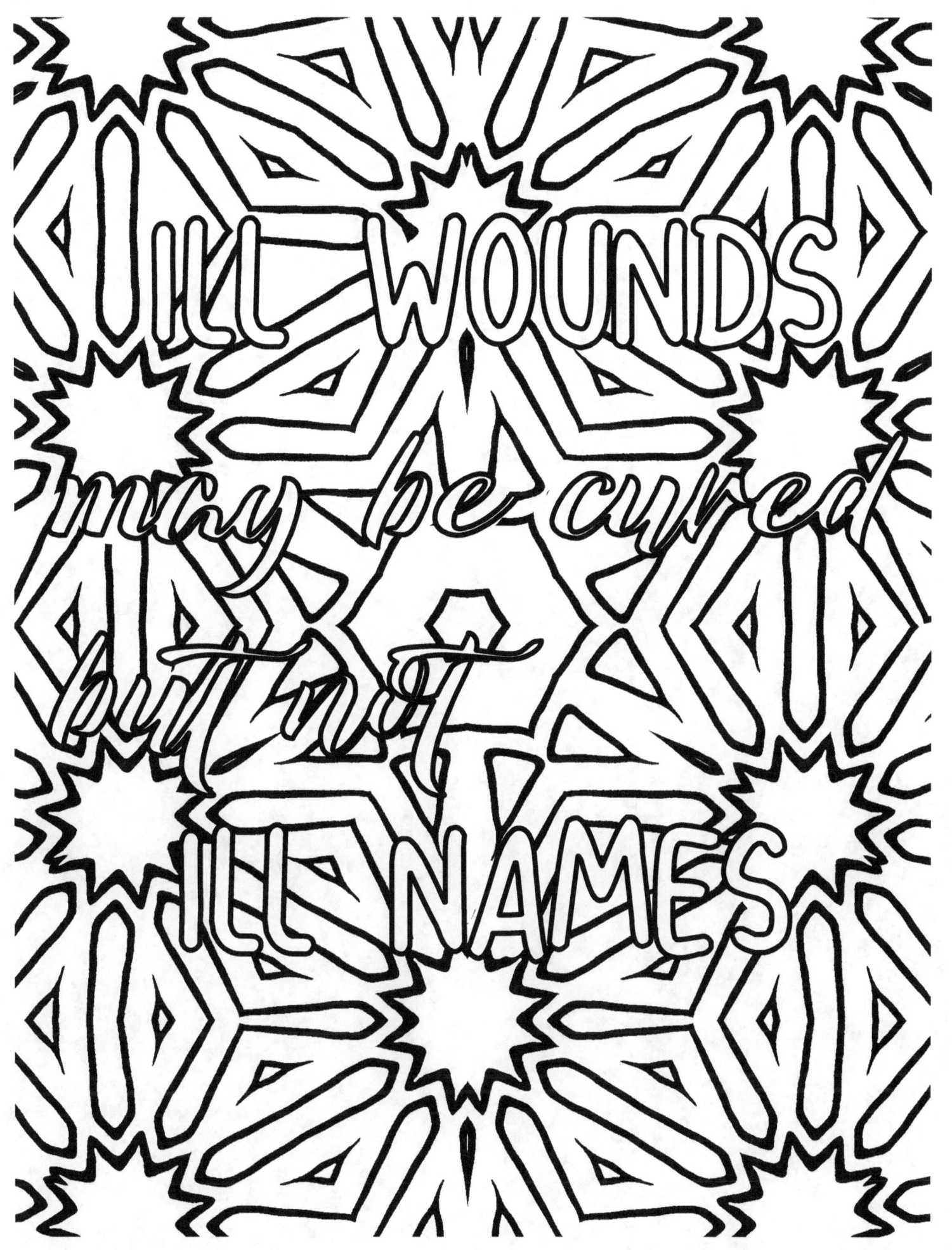

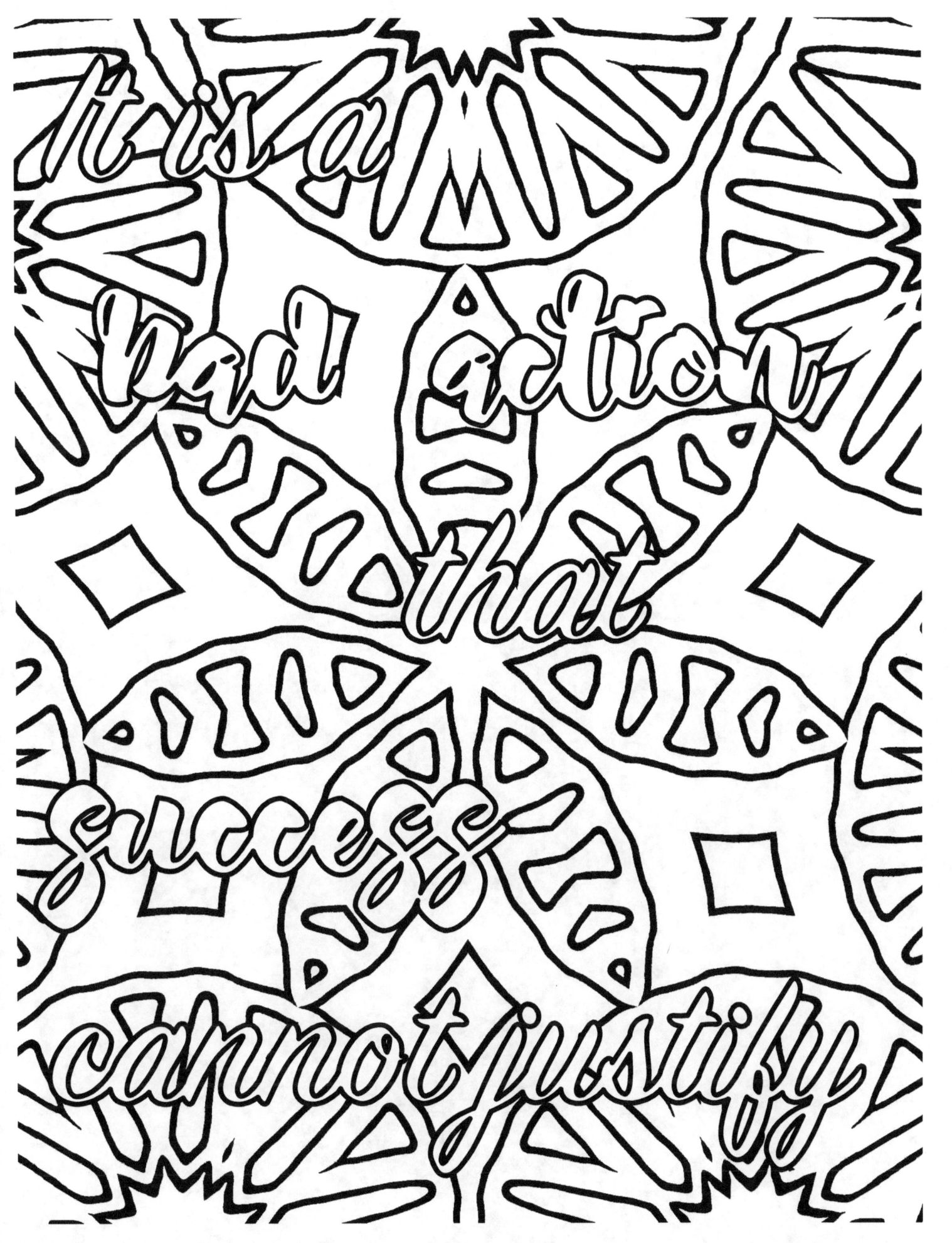

It is a bad action that success cannot justify

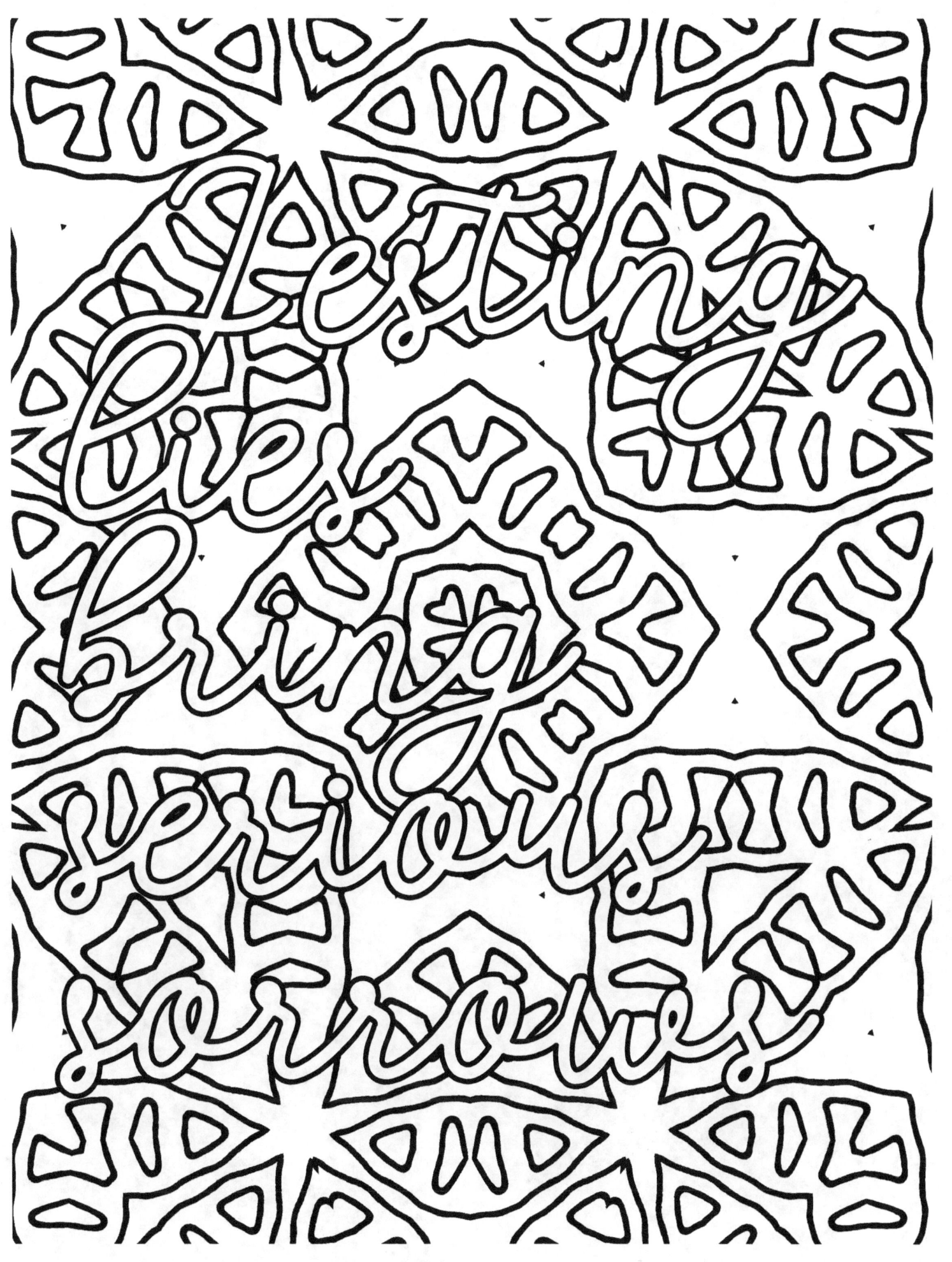

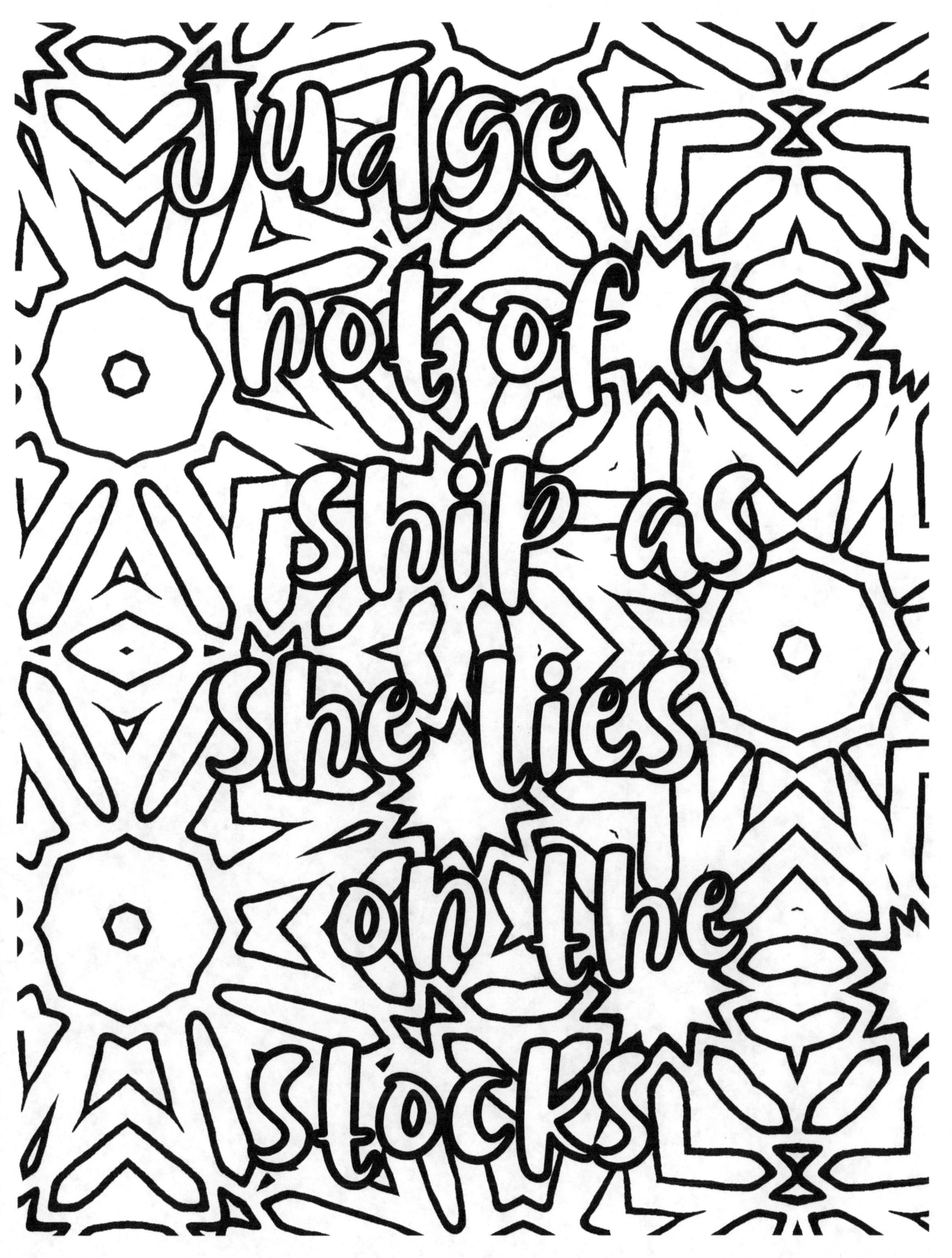

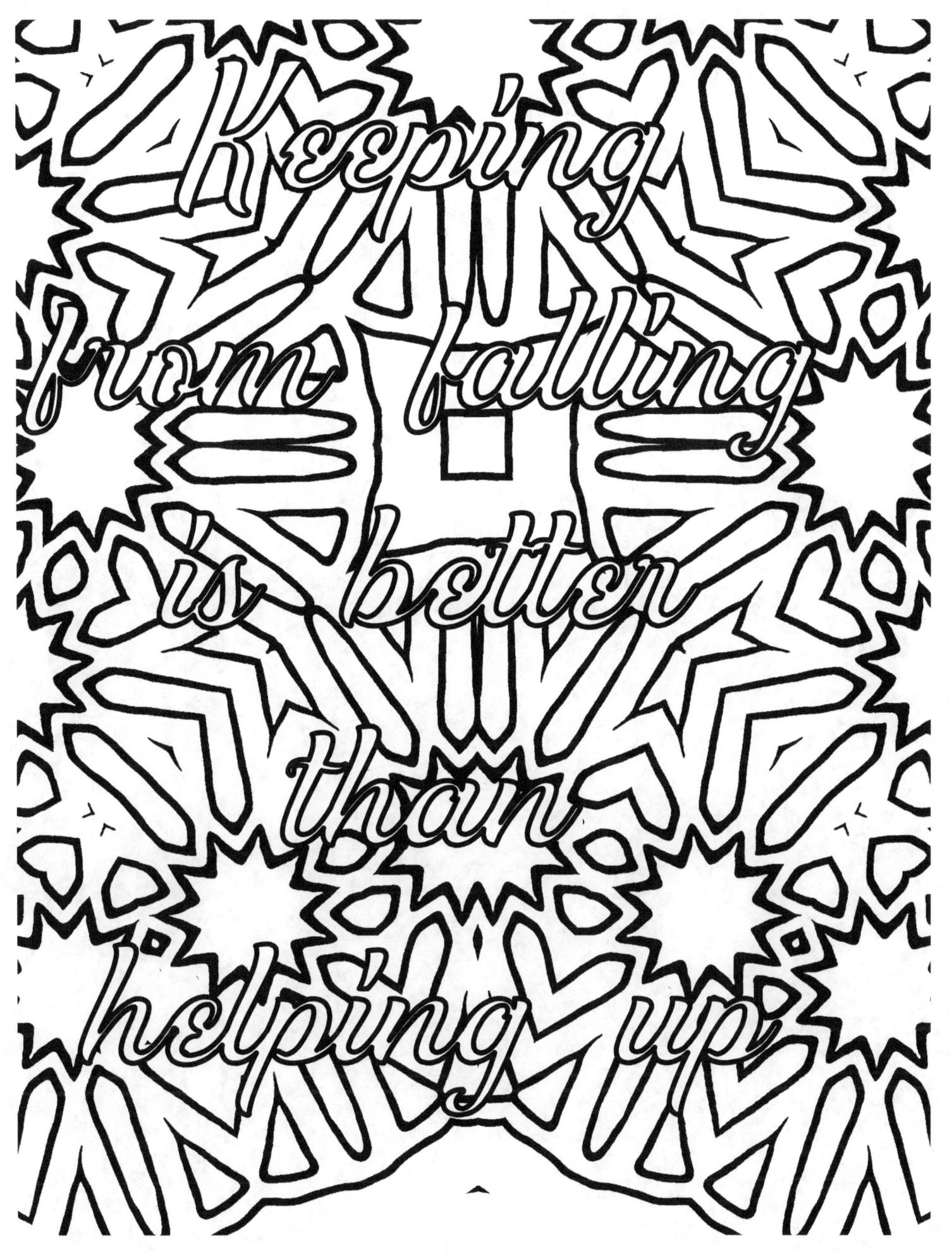

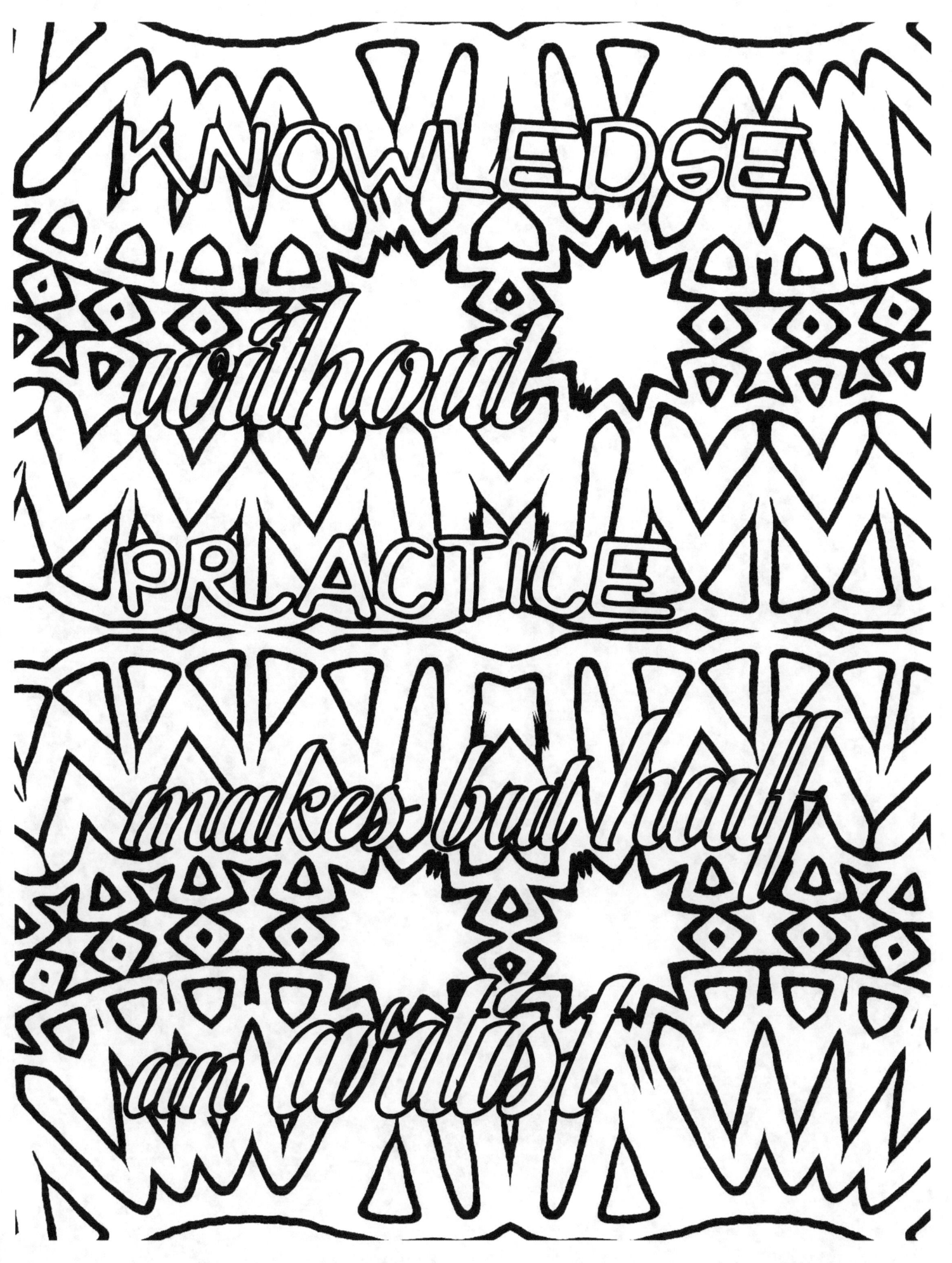

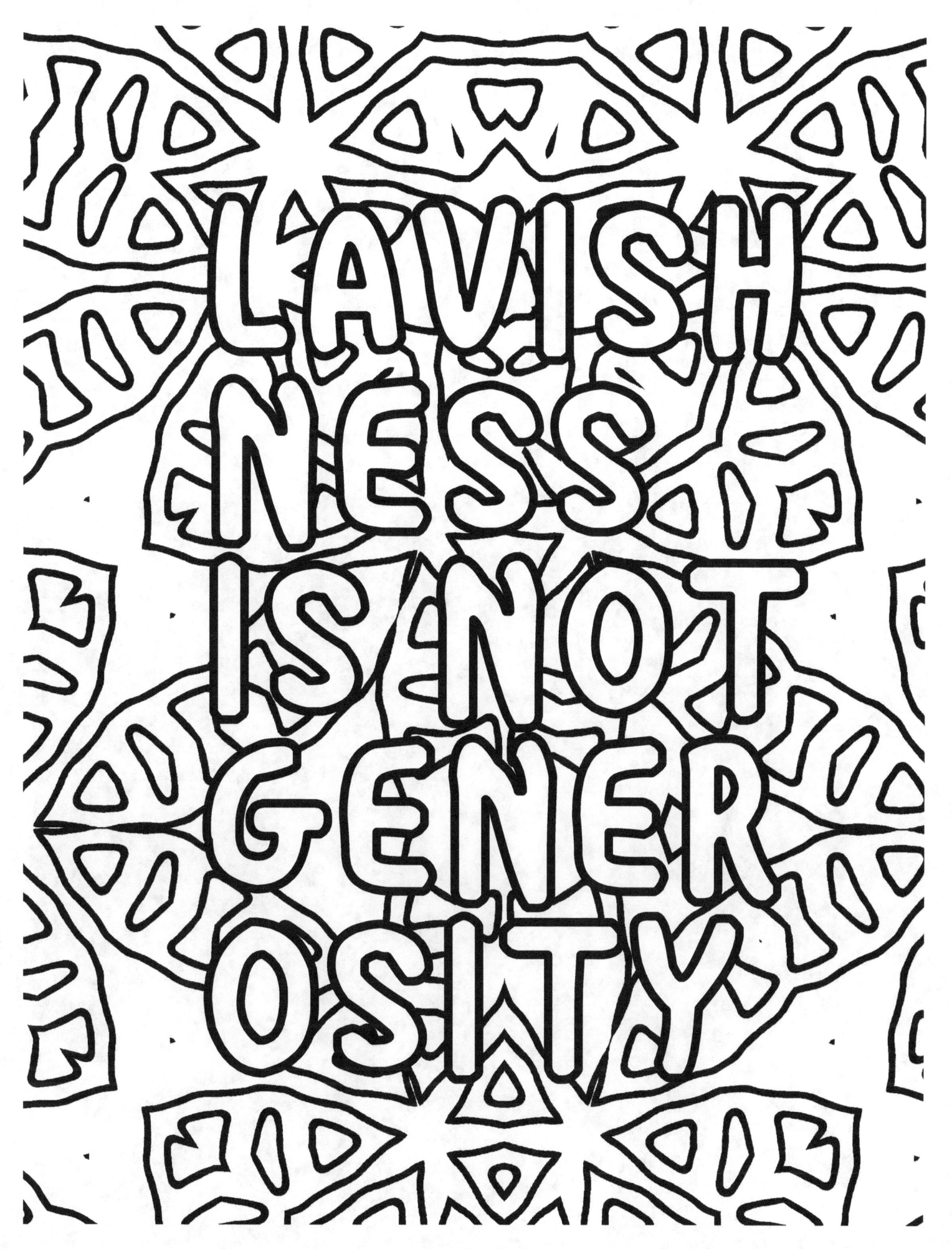

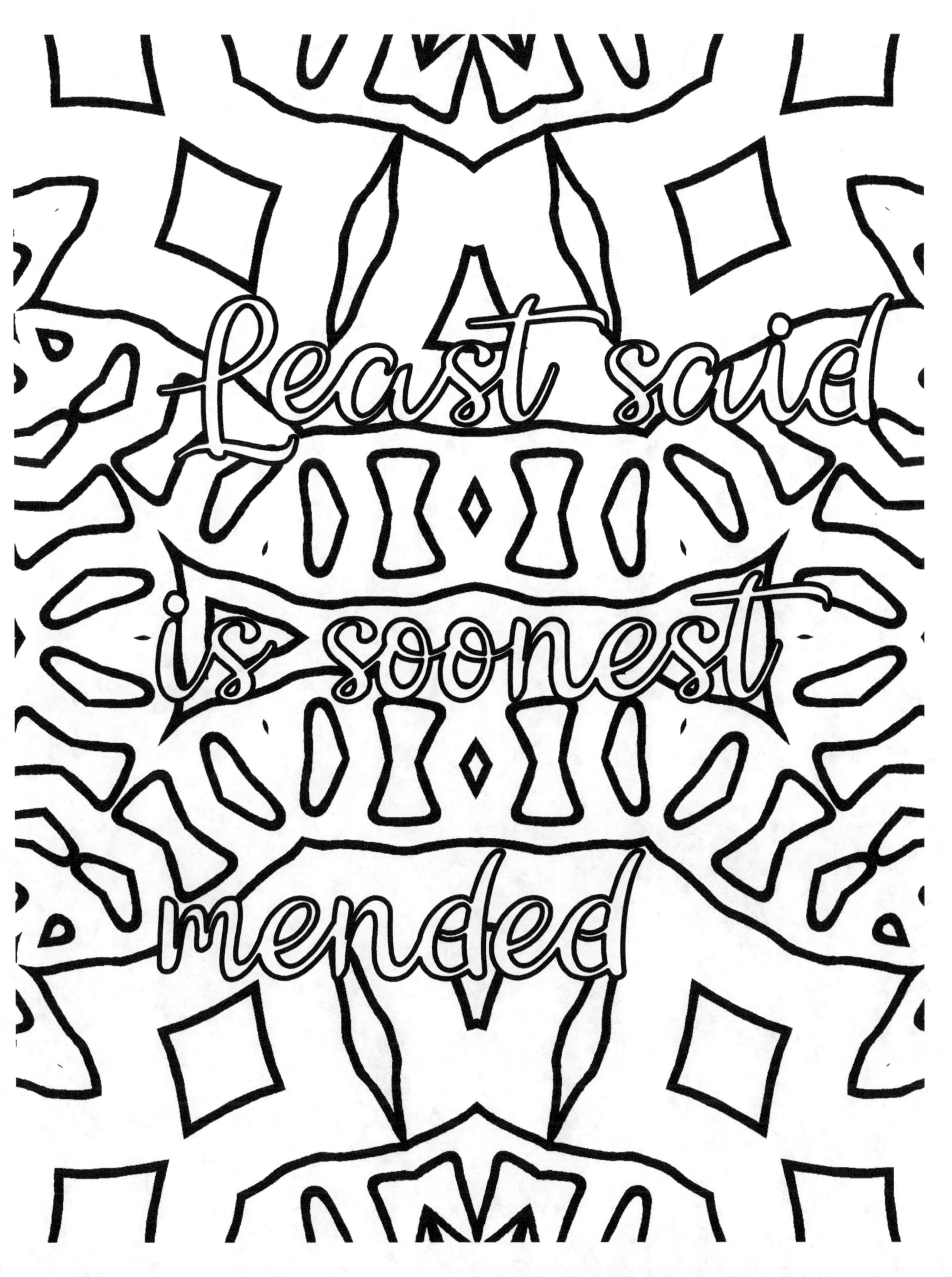

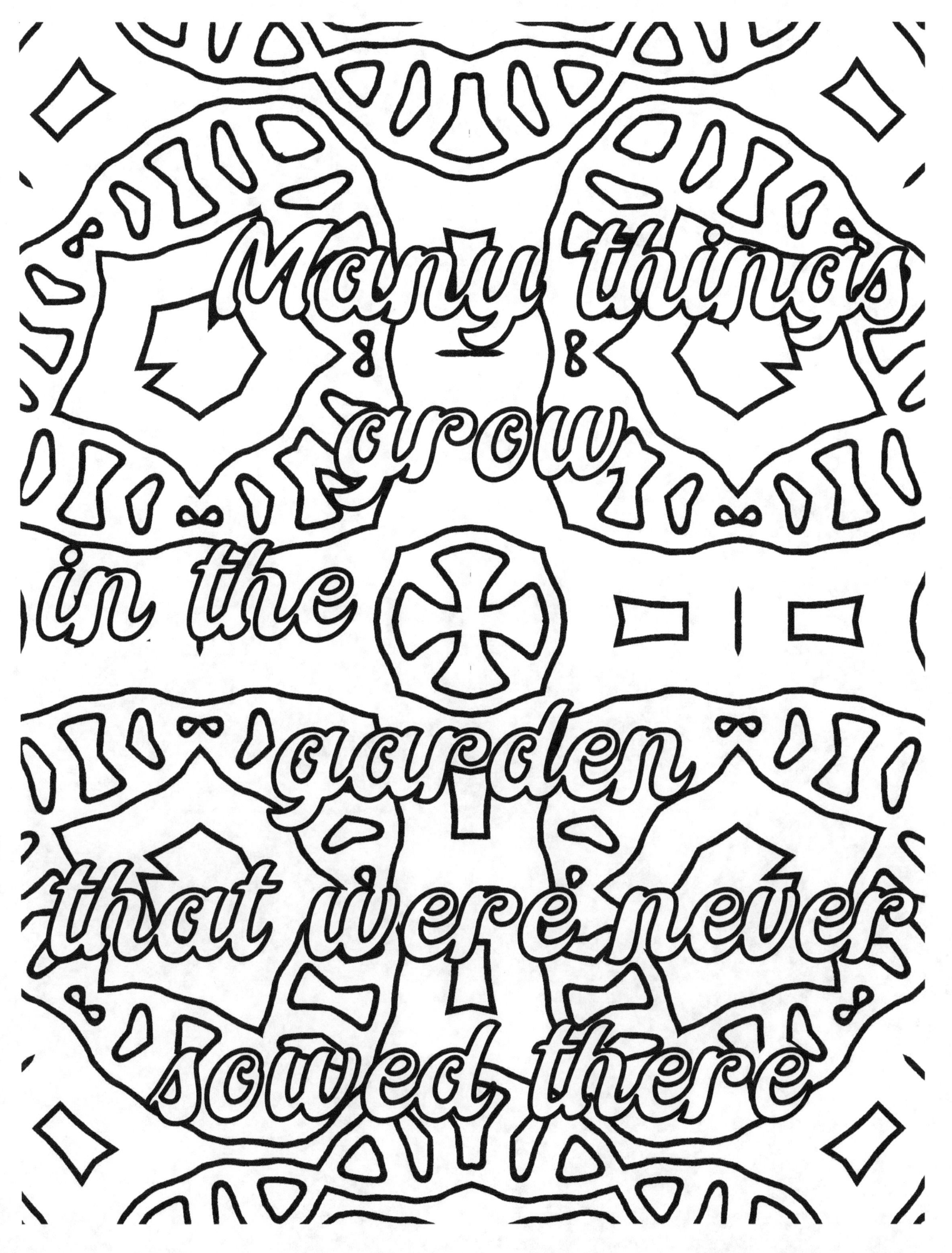

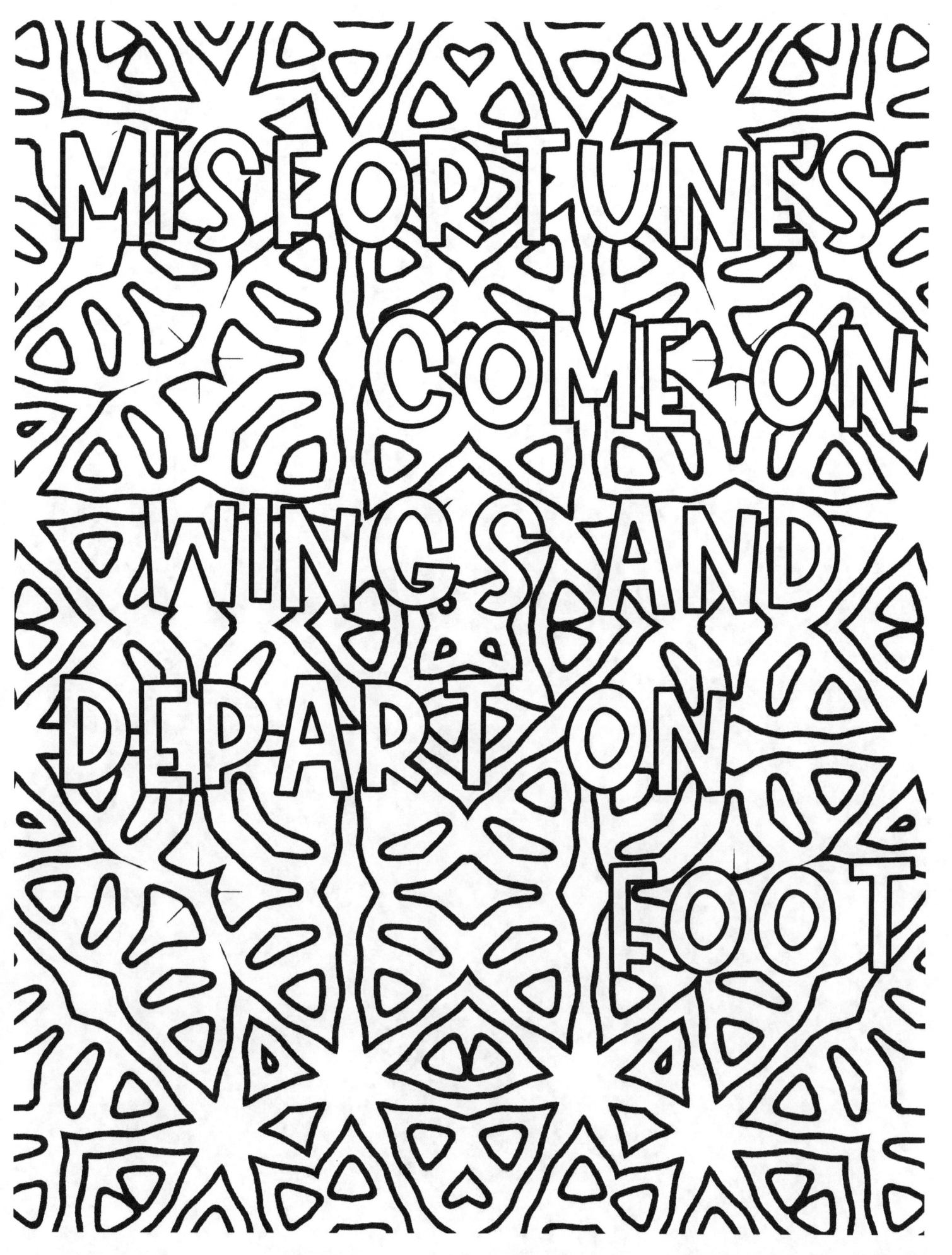

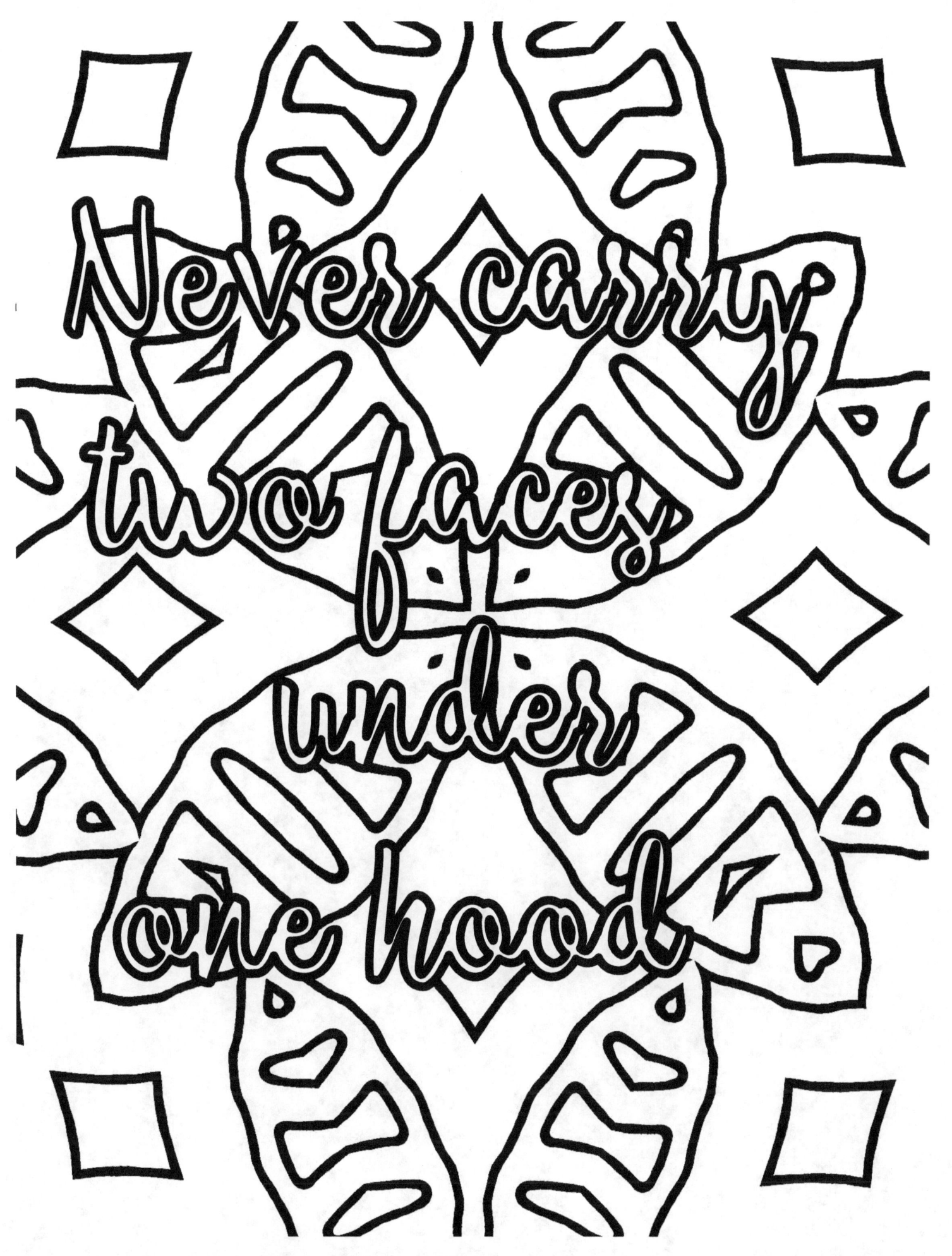

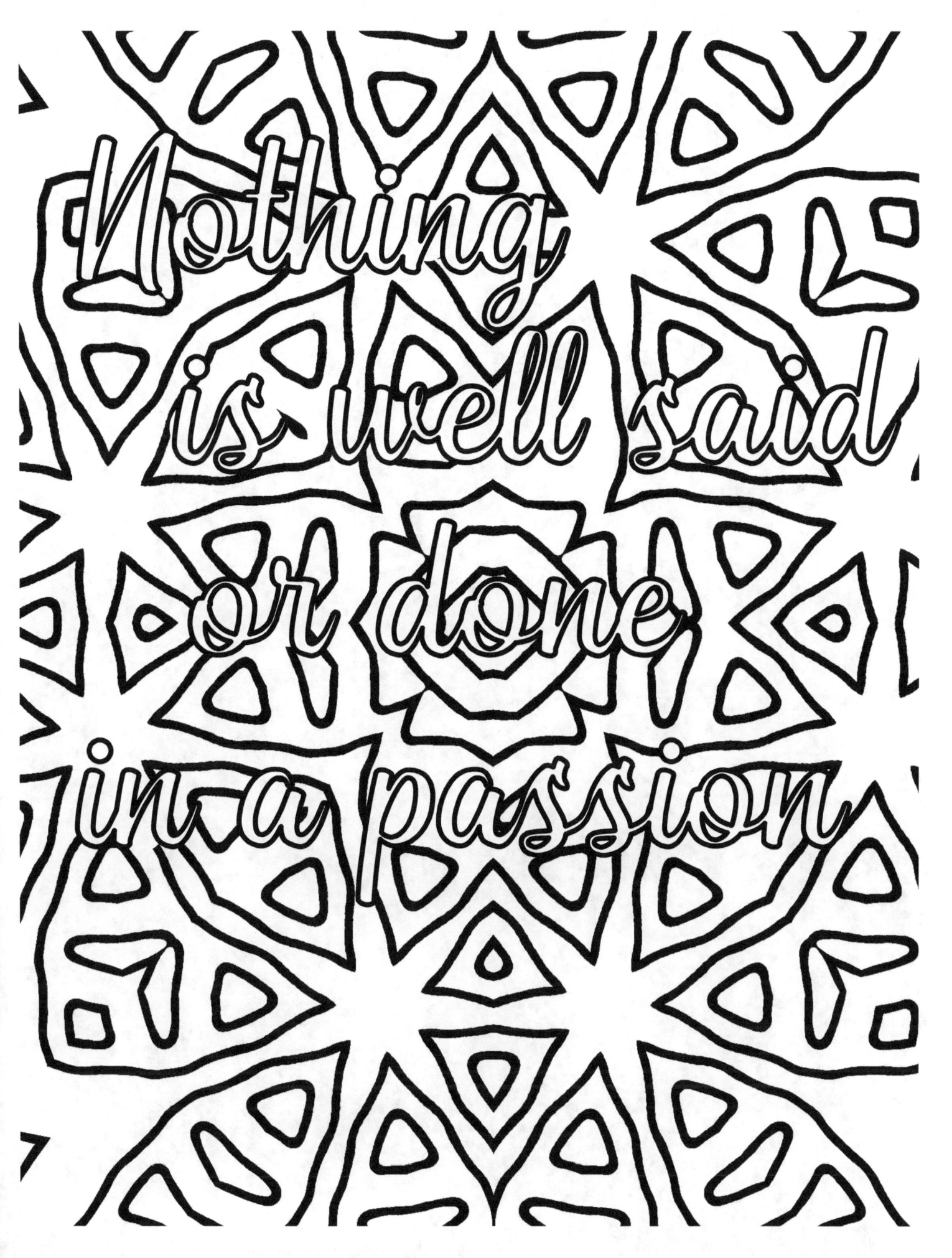

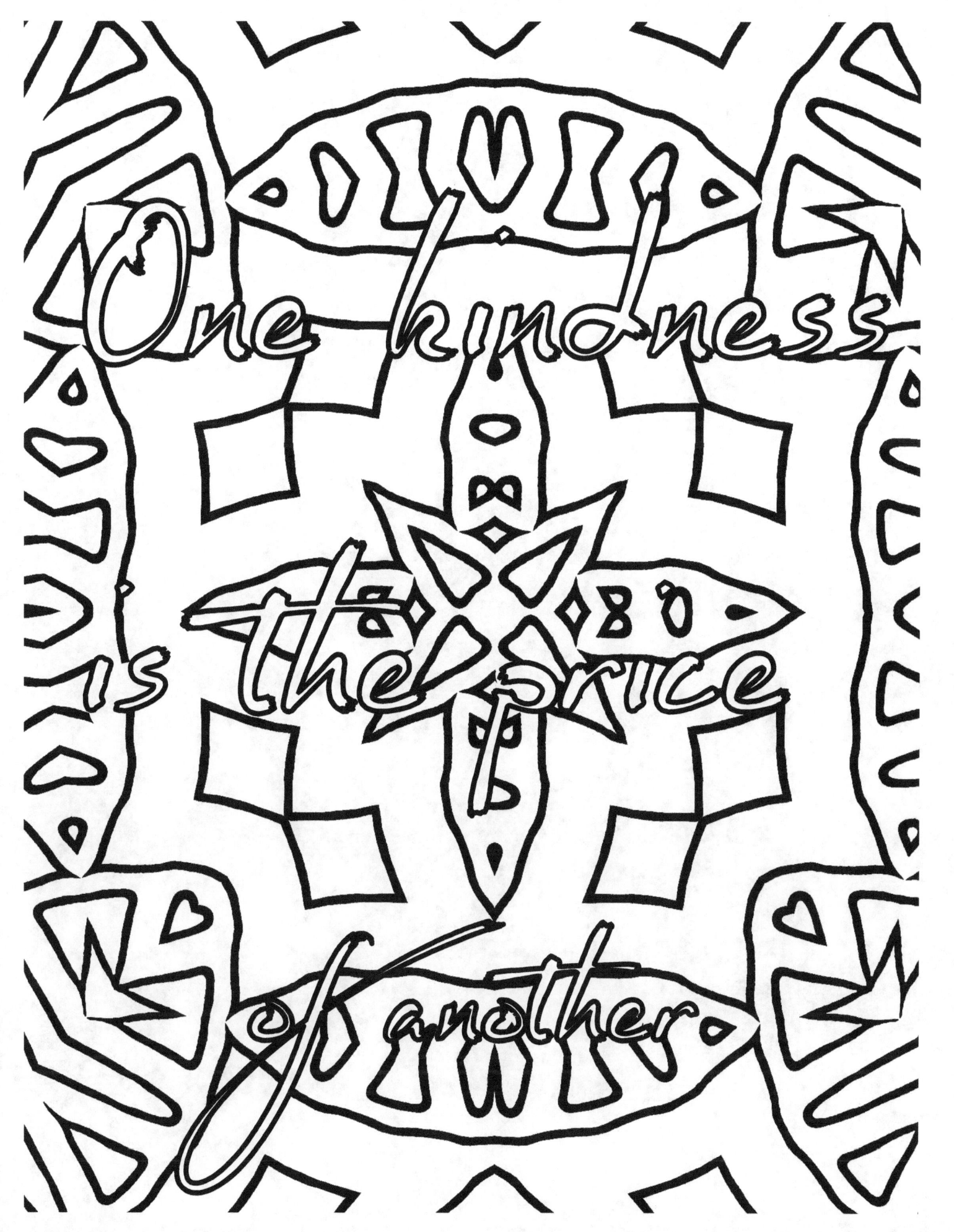

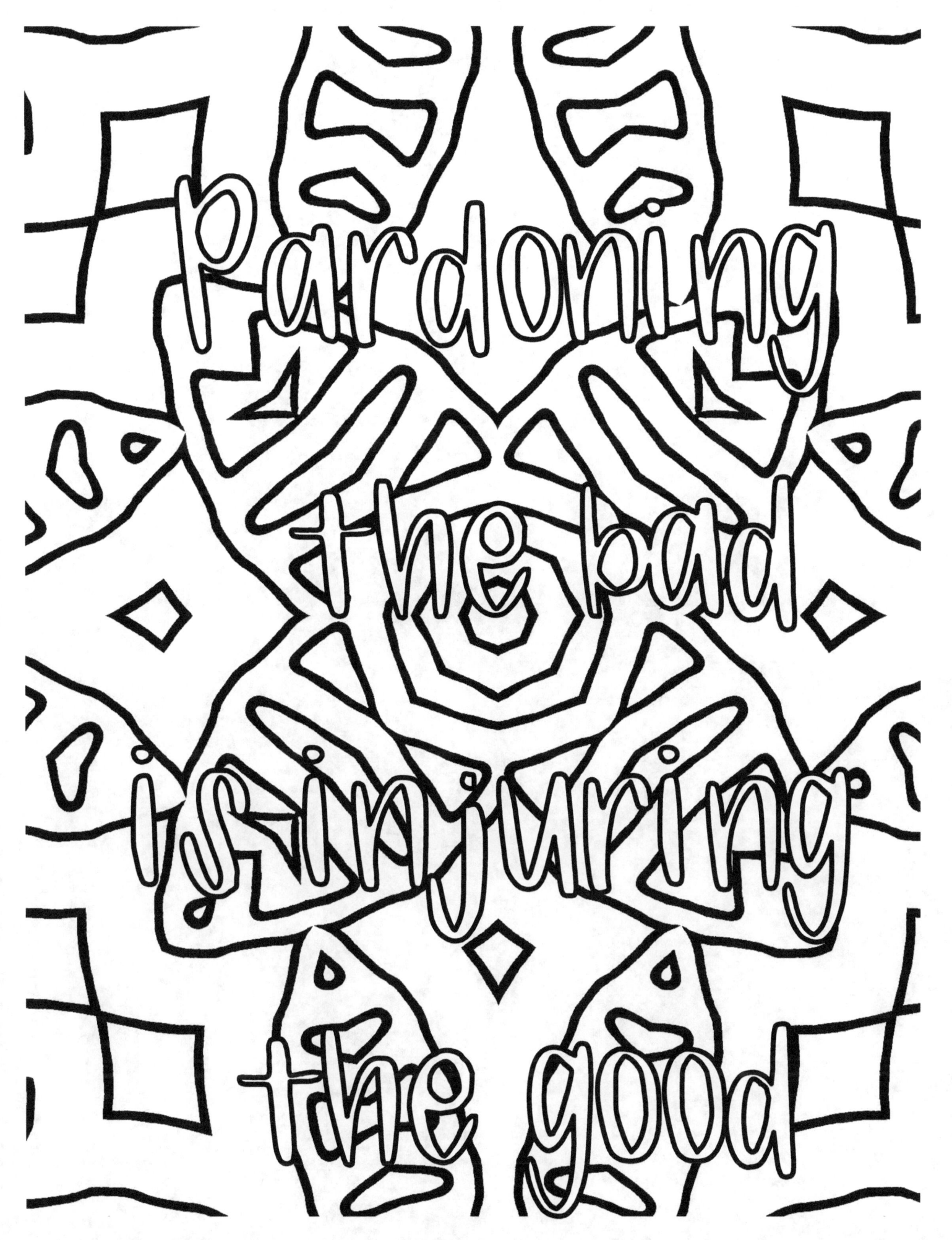

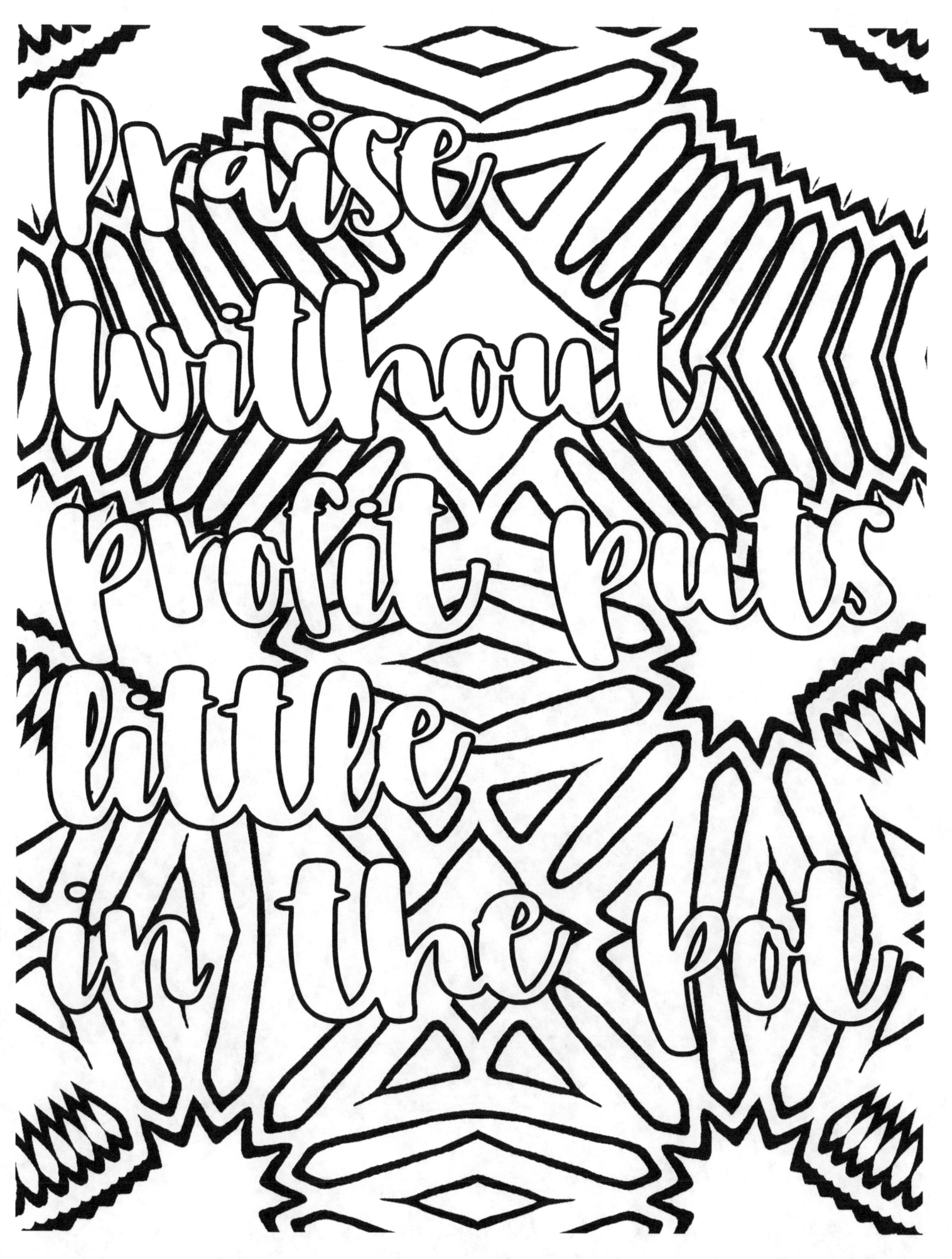

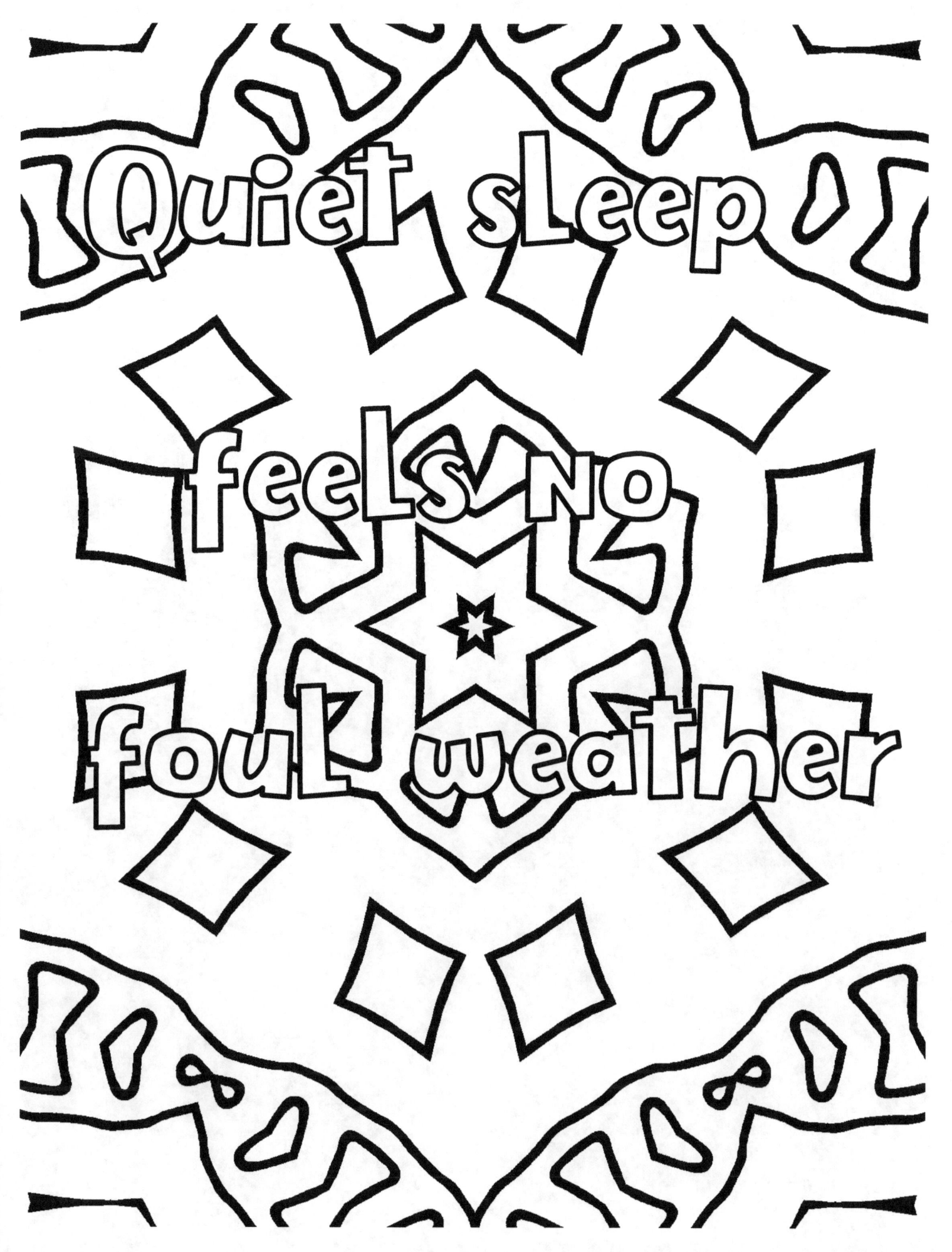

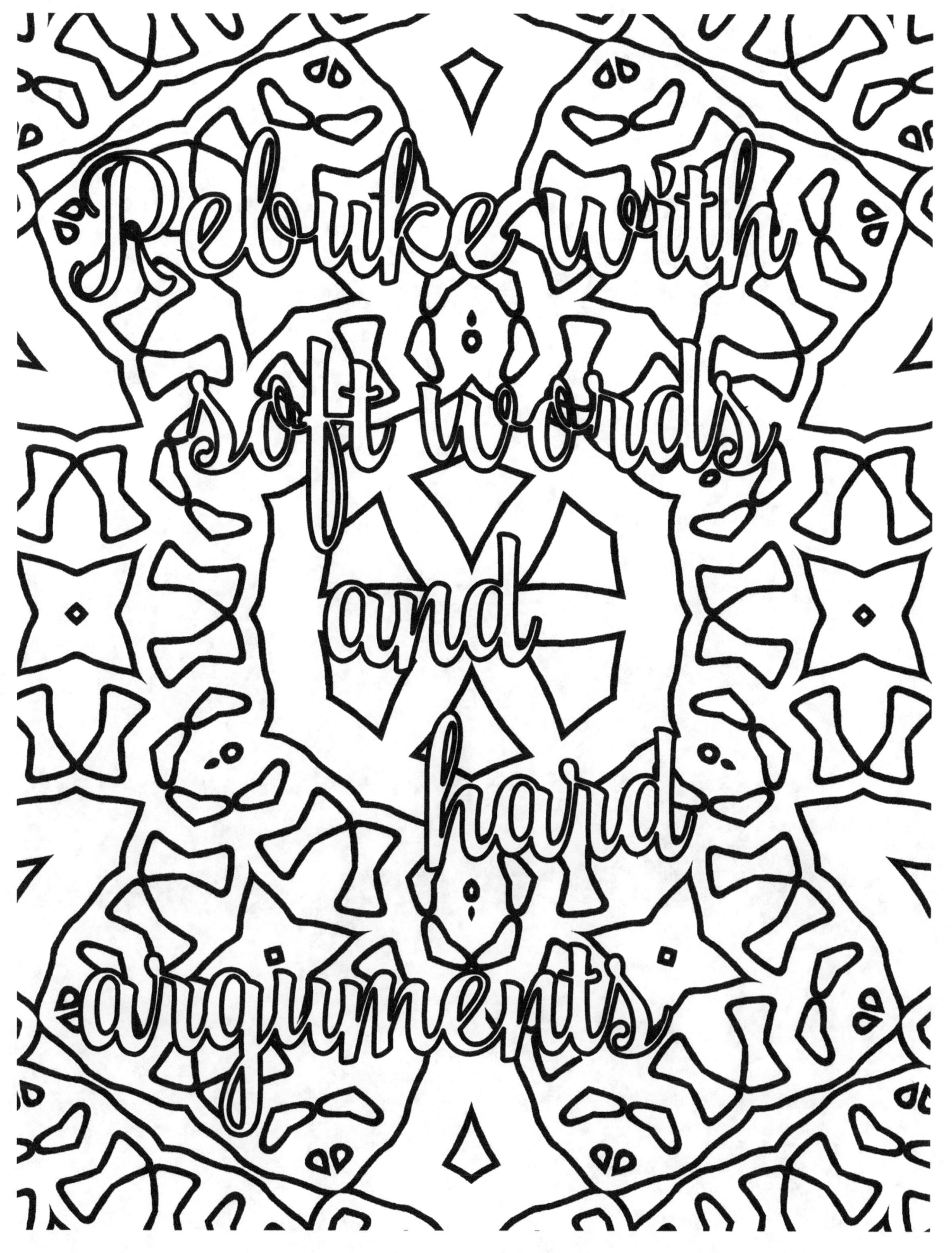

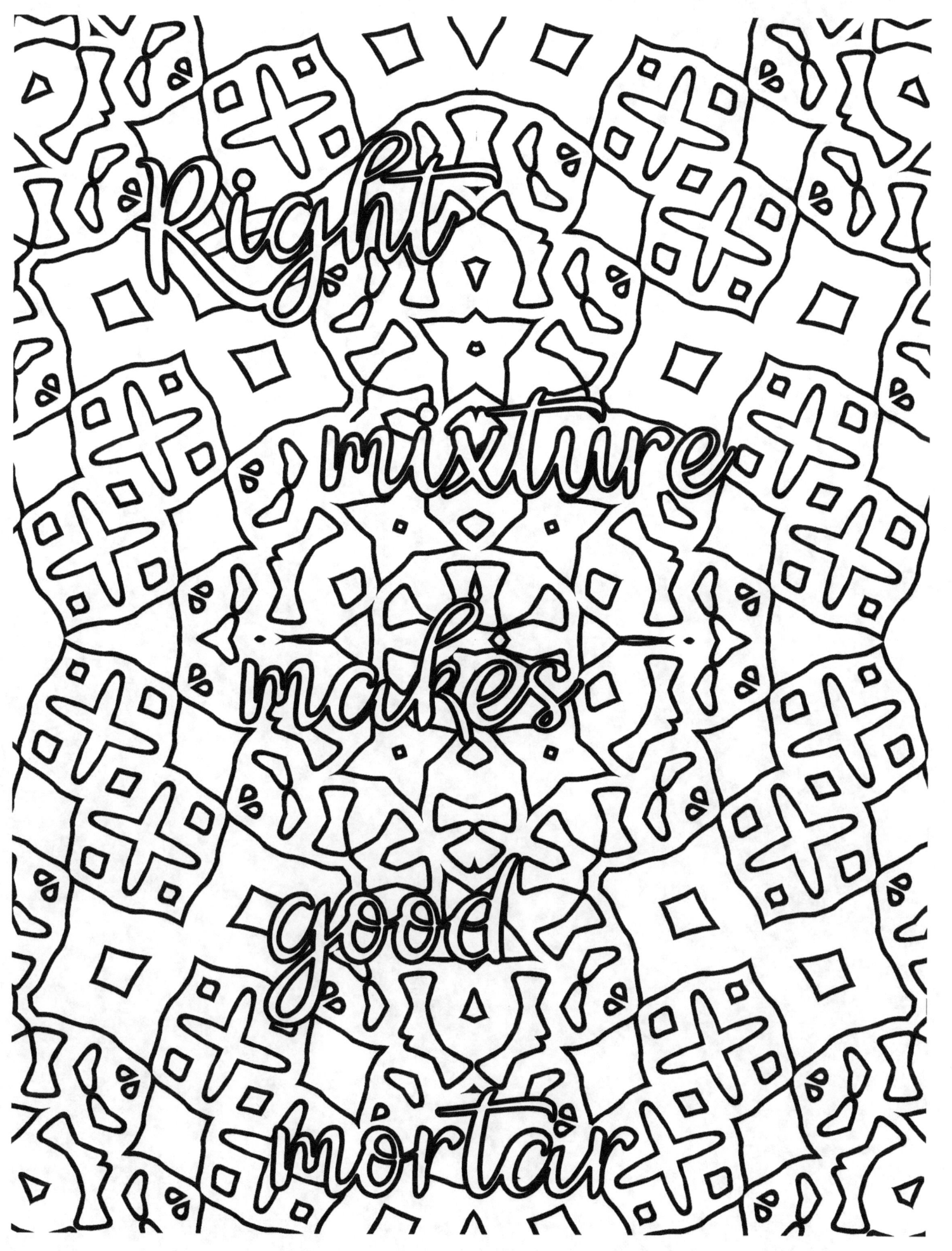

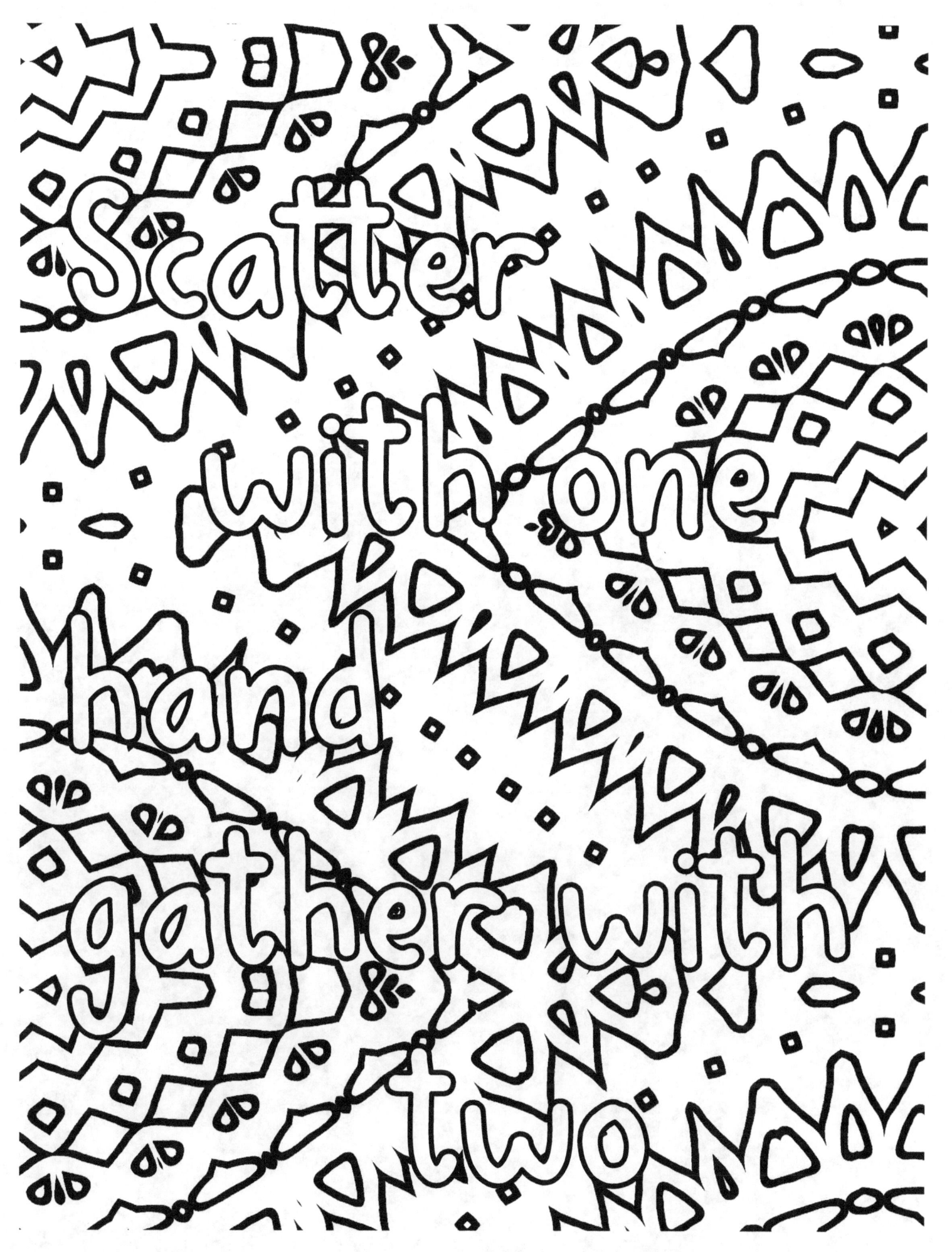

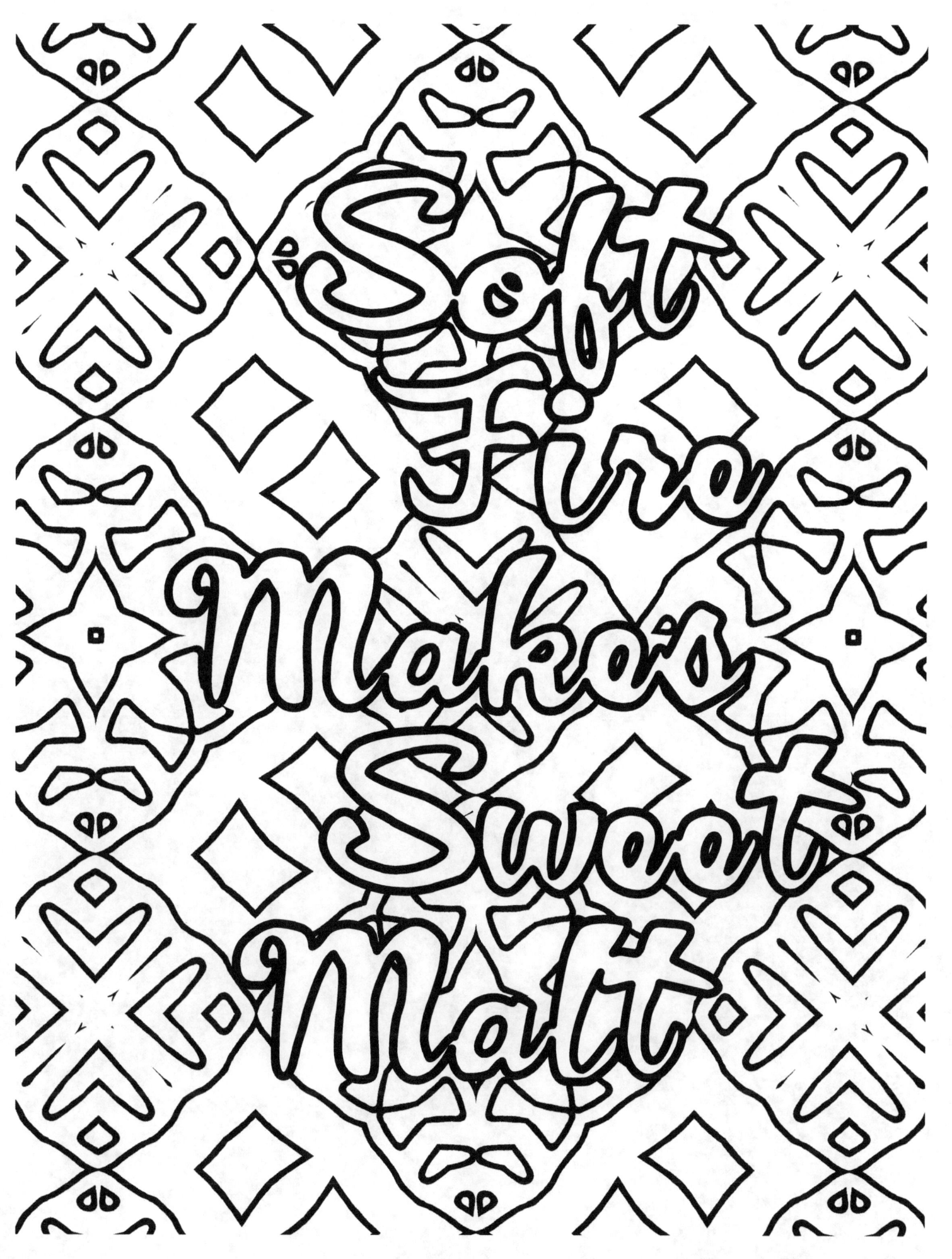

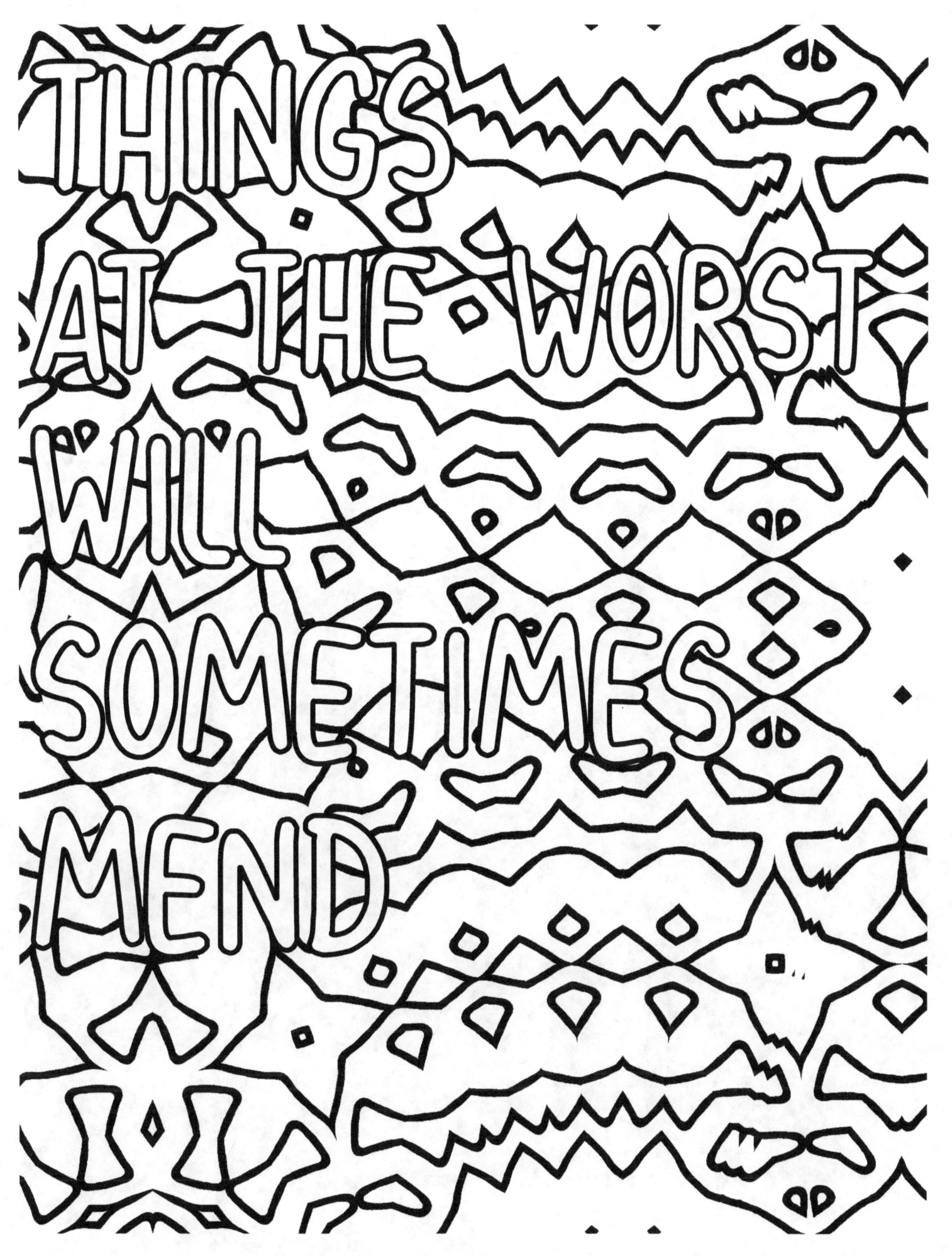

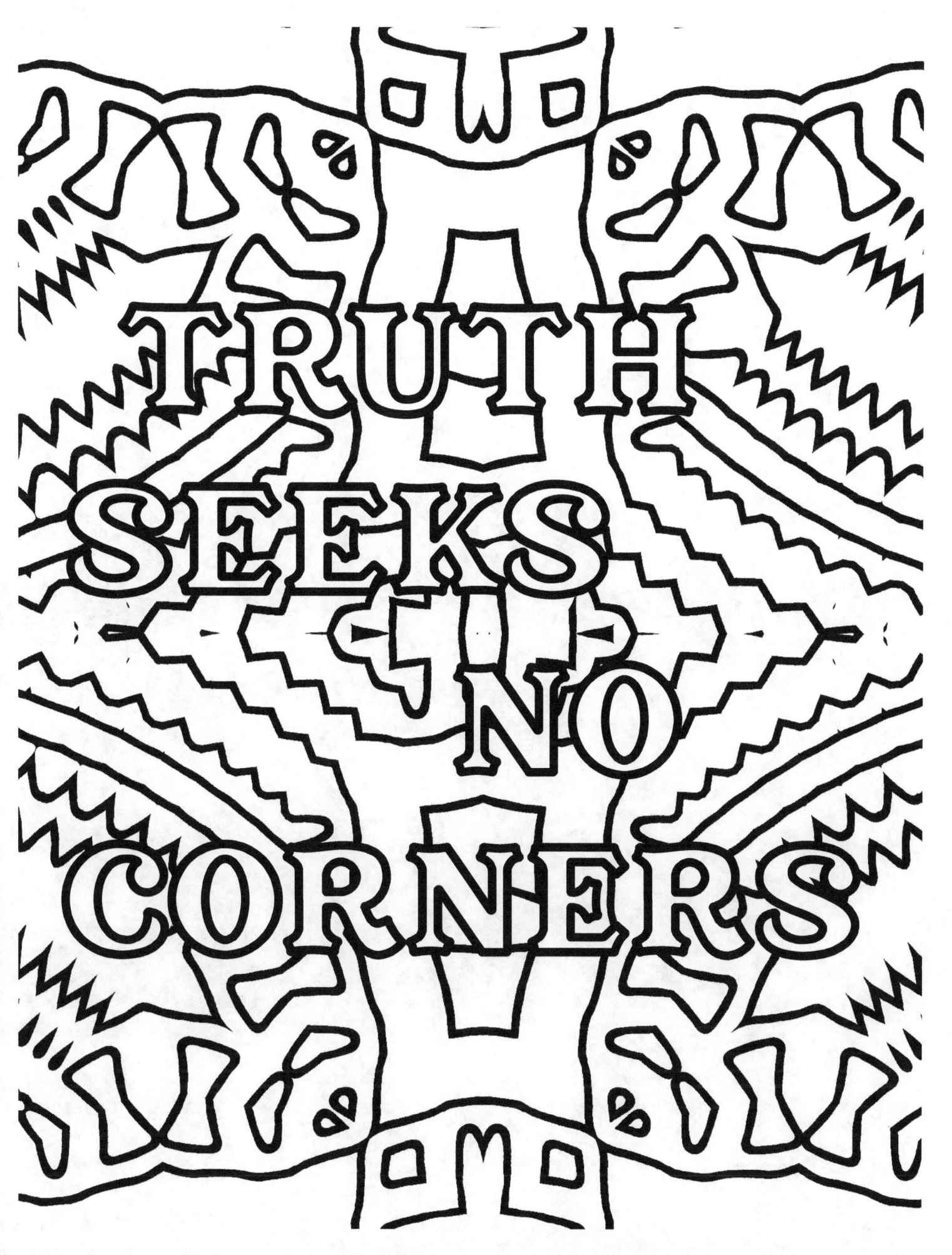

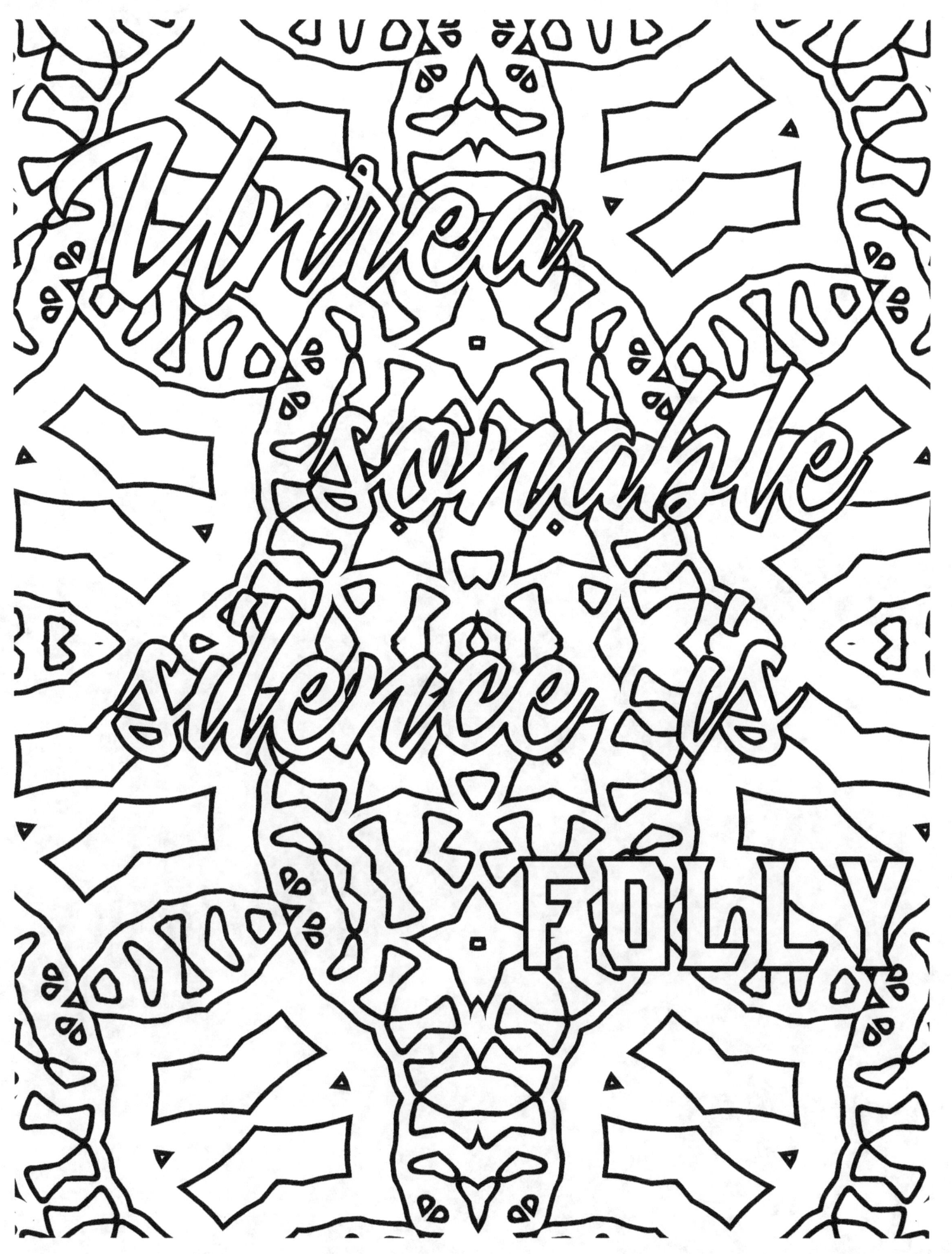

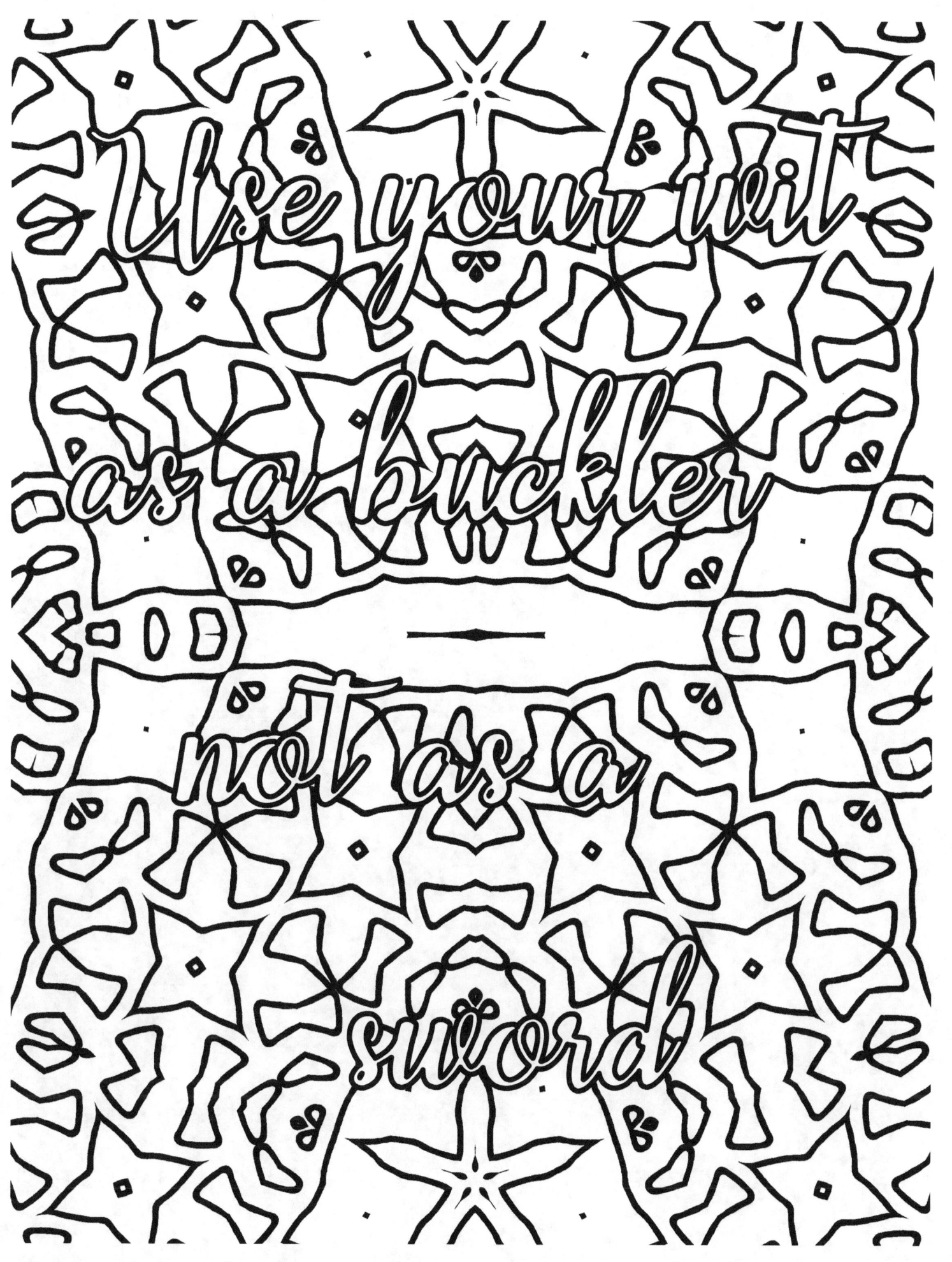

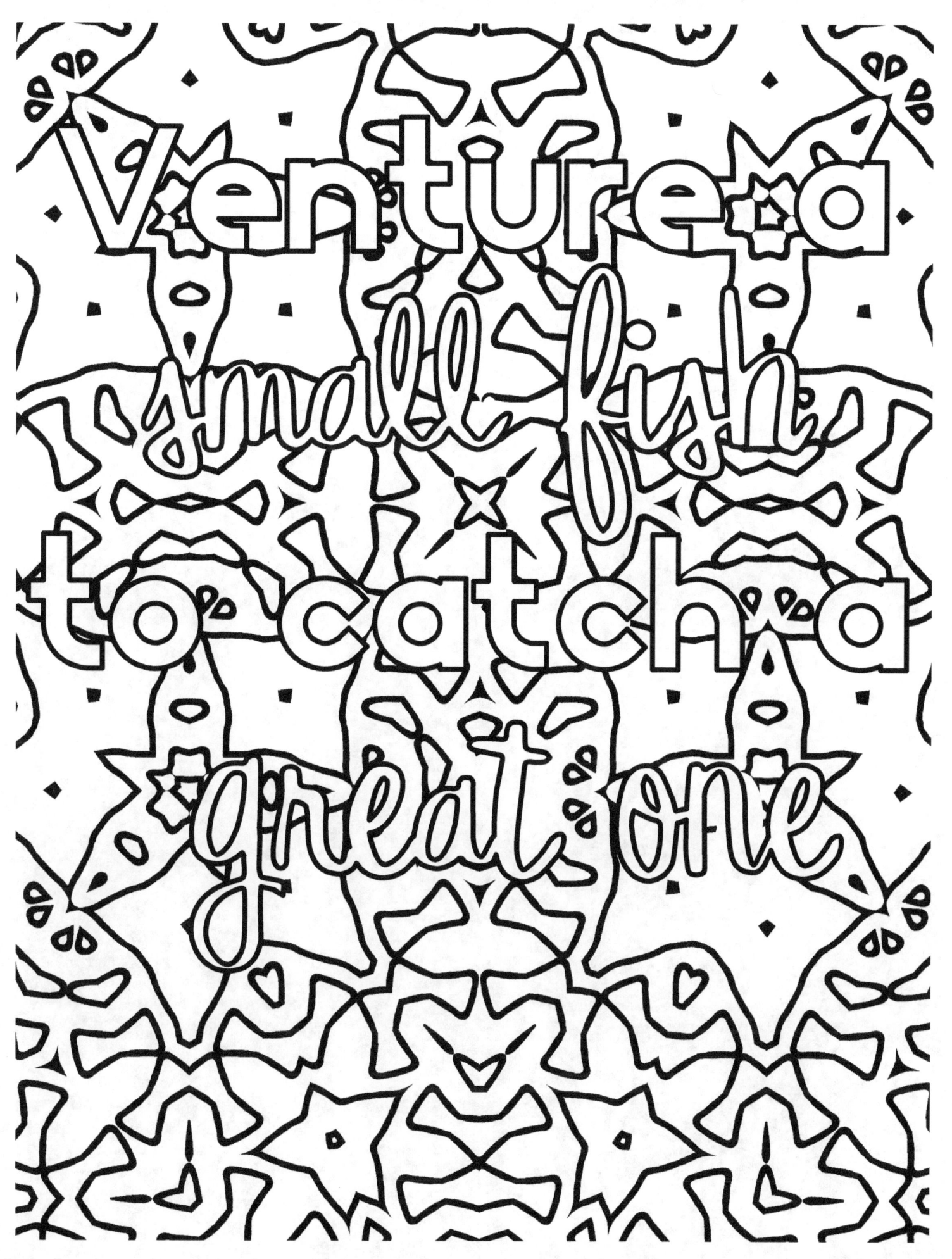

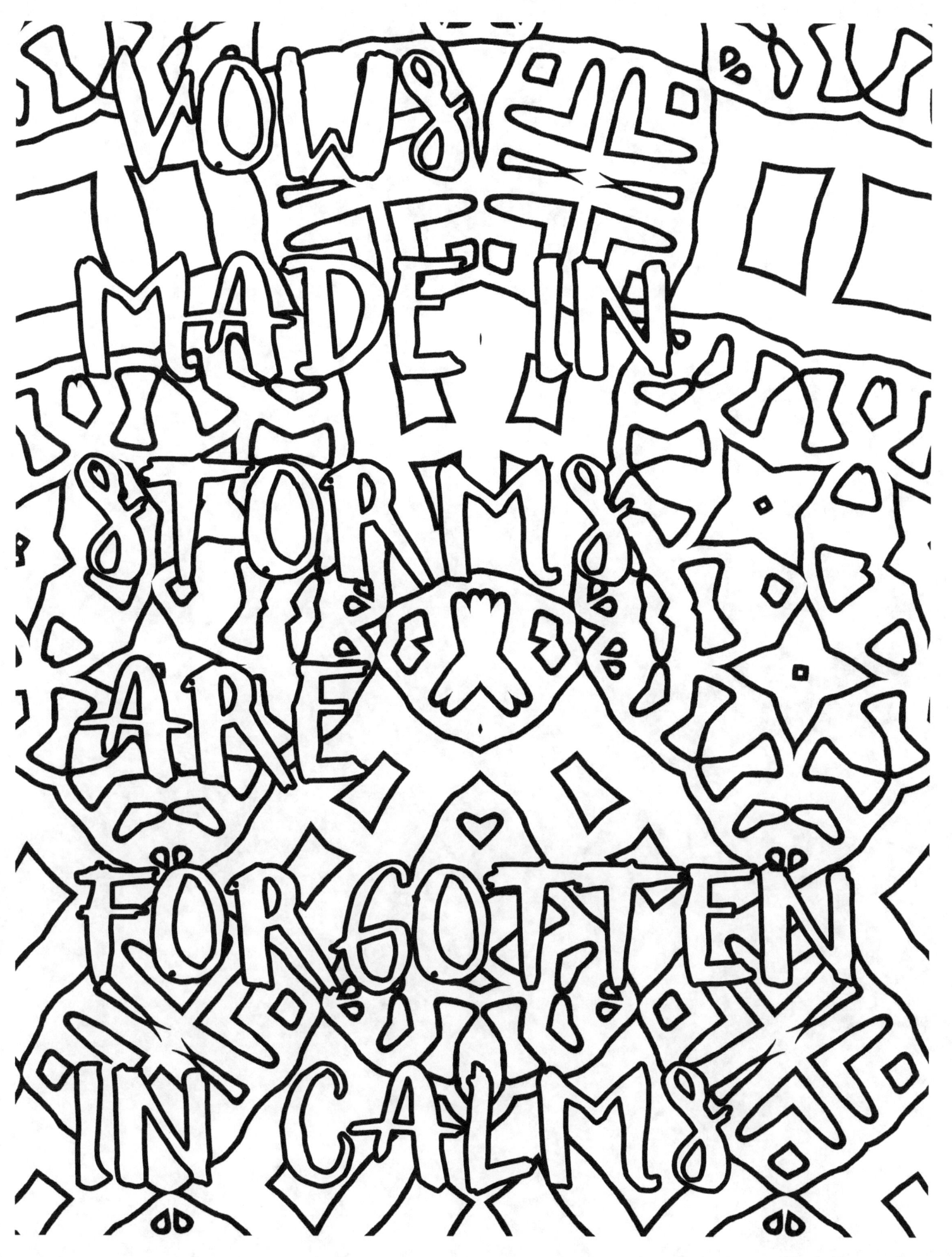

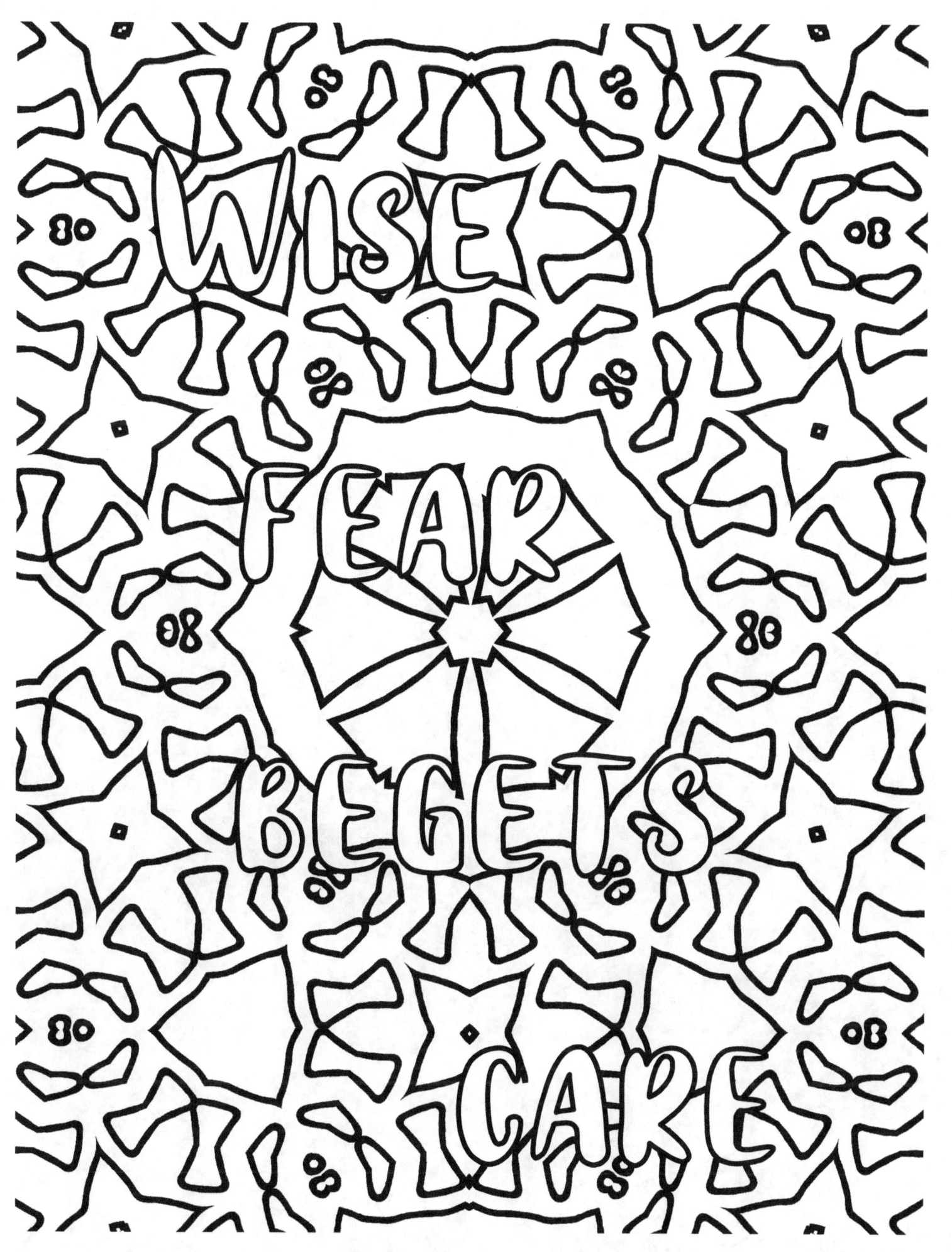

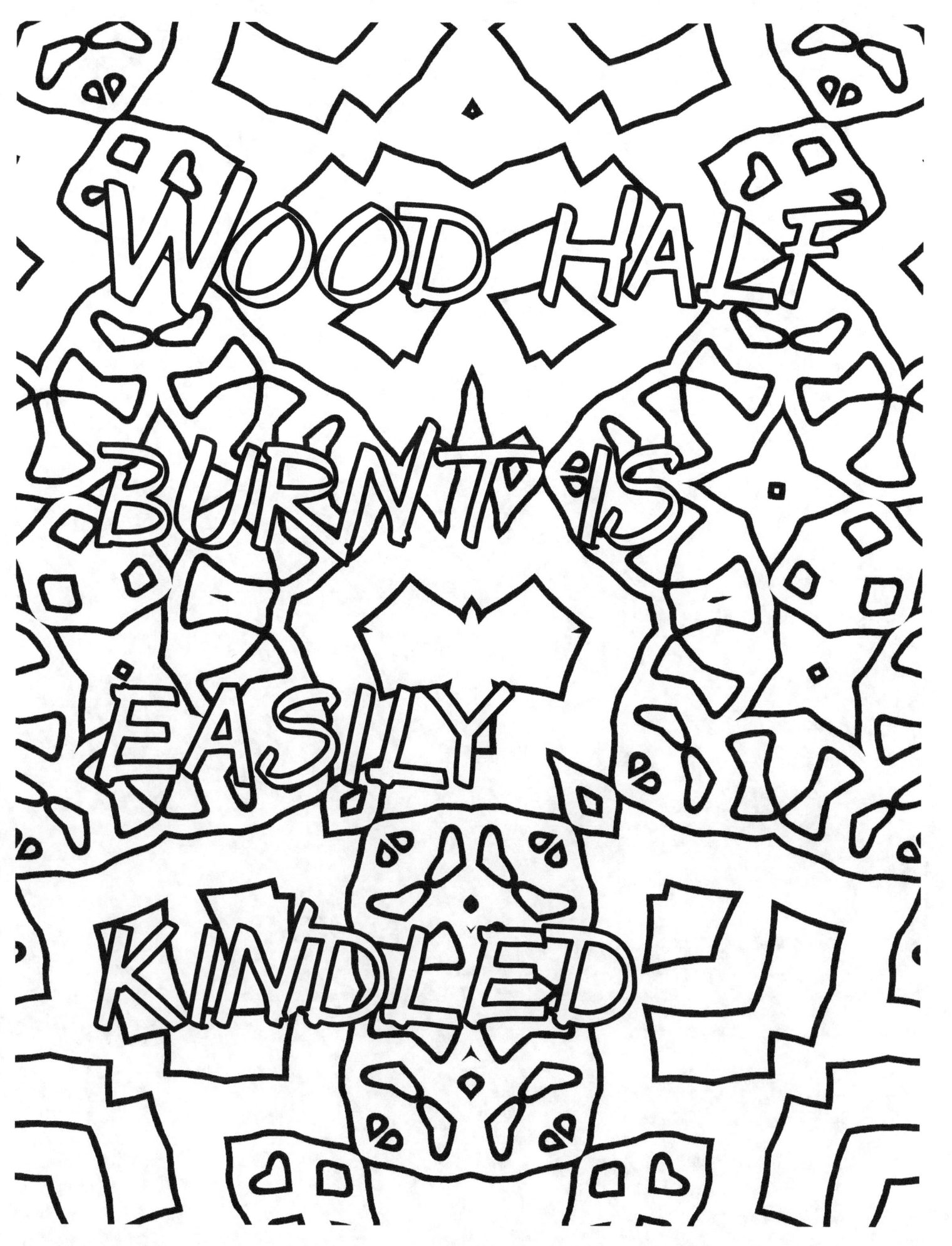

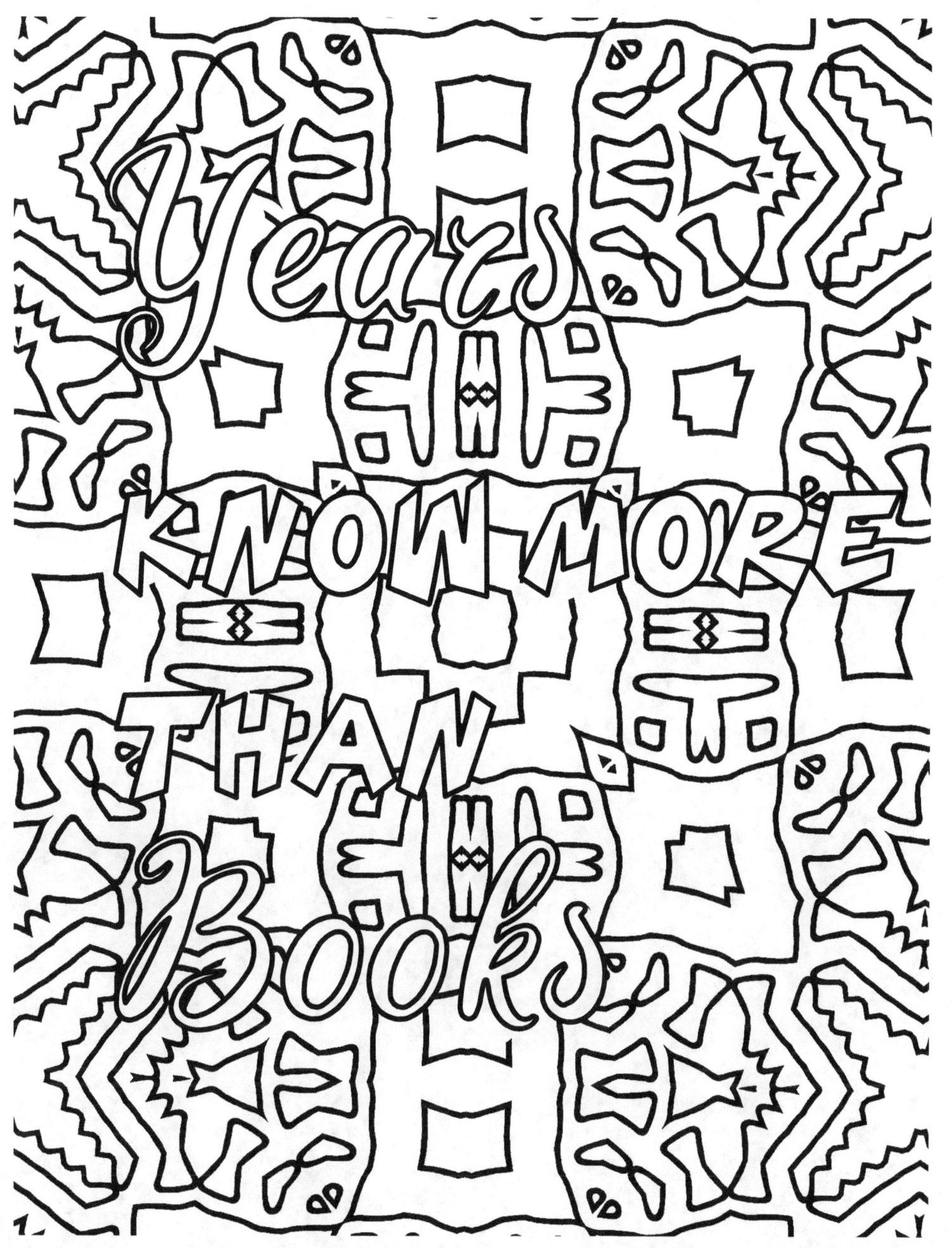

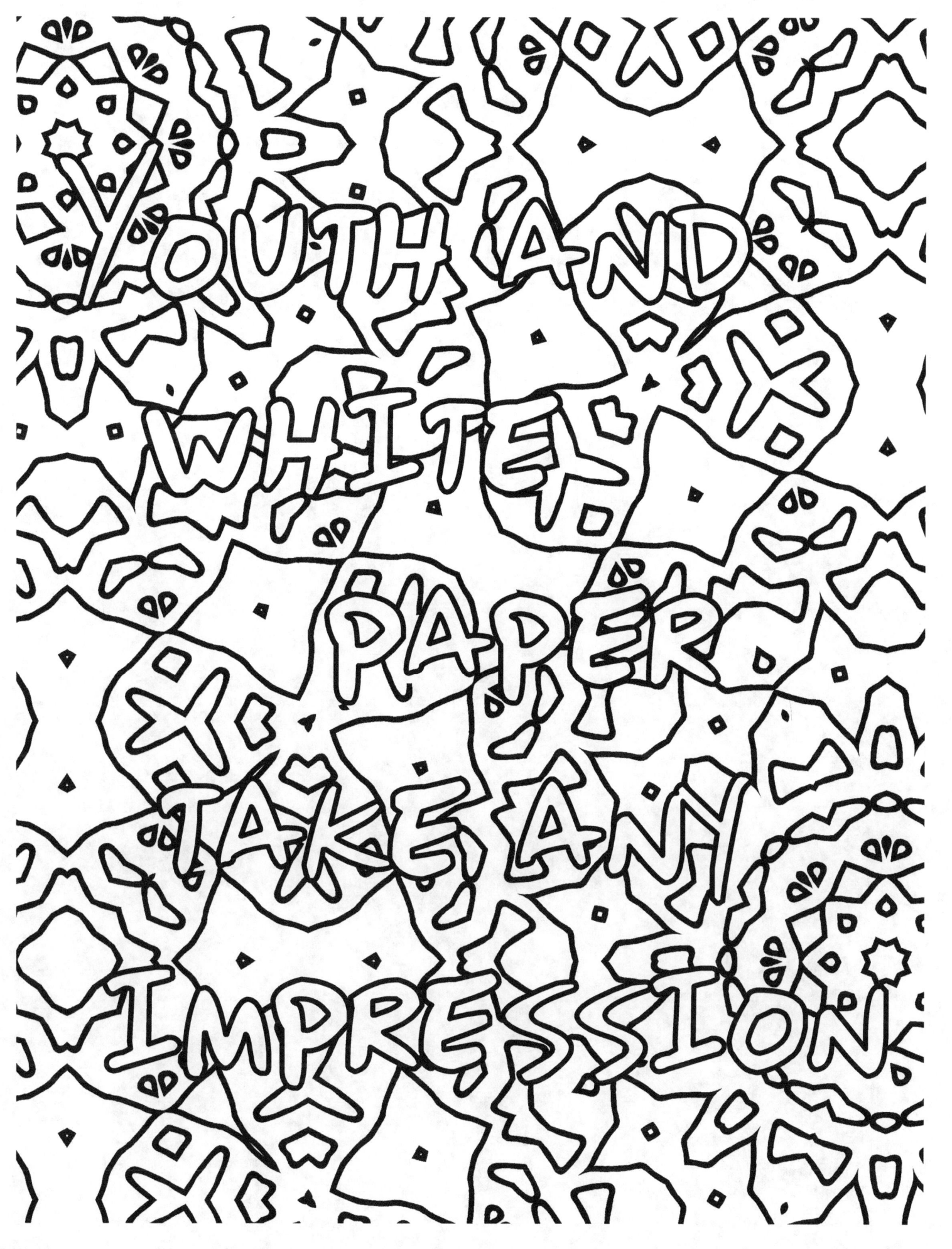

YOUTH AND WHITE PAPER TAKE ANY IMPRESSION

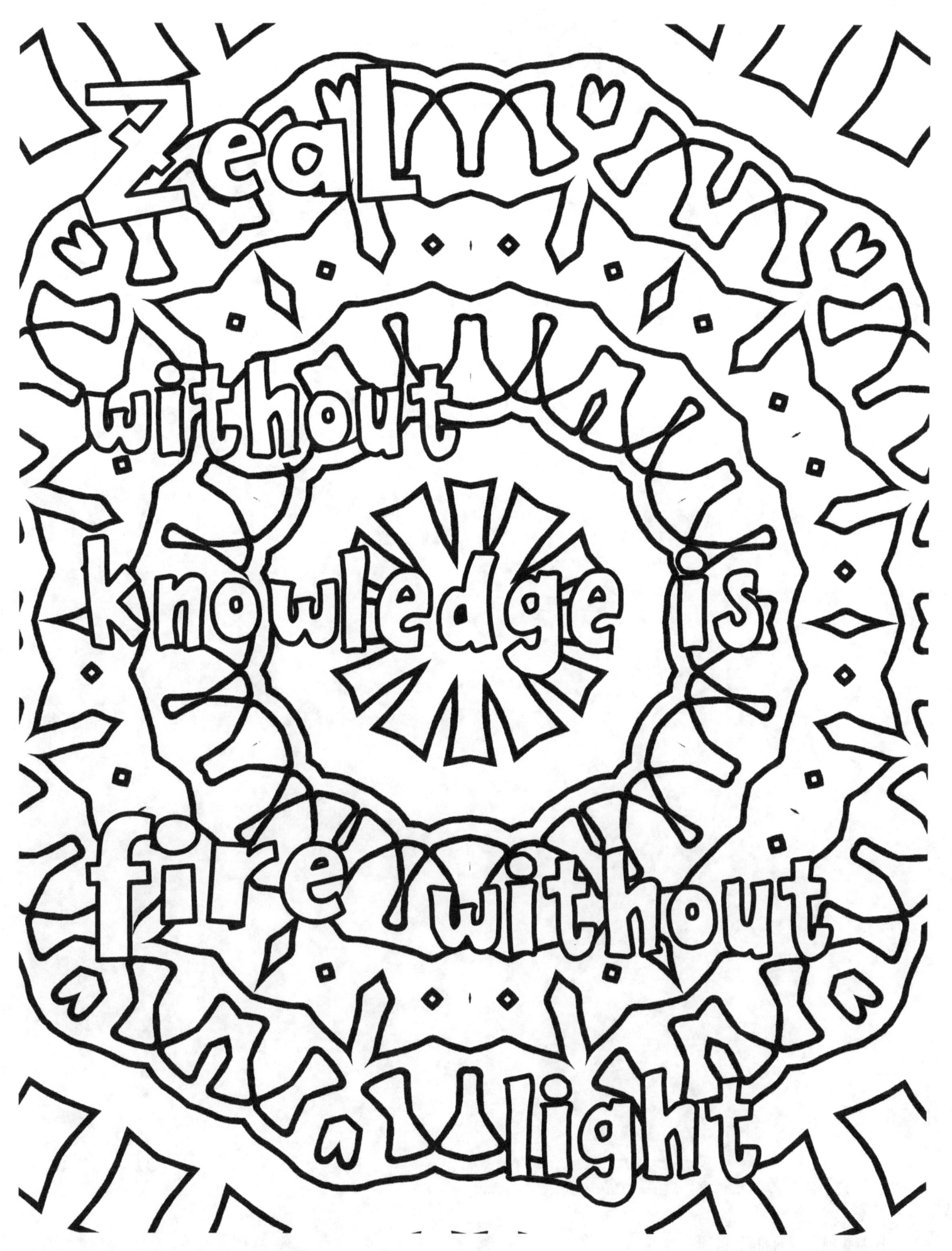

www.ingramcontent.com/pod-product-compliance
Lightning Source LLC
Chambersburg PA
CBHW080849220526
45467CB00008B/2448